THE SEARCH FOR MEANING

A New Approach in Psychotherapy

by

A. J. UNGERSMA

Foreword by Viktor E. Frankl

THE WESTMINSTER PRESS

Philadelphia

To Mary and Mike
Companions in Vienna

Published by The Westminster Press ®
Philadelphia, Pennsylvania

PRINTED IN THE UNITED STATES OF AMERICA

Foreword

The author's wish that I write this foreword to his book is gladly fulfilled because, if there is anything such as a truly American pioneering spirit still alive, and more specifically, if this spirit is operant in the field of psychotherapy, it must indeed have been at work in Professor Ungersma. For he is to be credited with having been the first American professor to spend a sabbatical year in Vienna for study of logotherapy at first hand.

The present book comes out of his work with us in the Neurological Polyclinic of Vienna. It still evokes the vivid experience of our mutual encounter. But it also conveys the warm humanness of its author who is a gifted and talented counselor. As such he must early have come across the frustration of " the search for meaning," to quote the title of this book. And as a counselor who holds his hand on the pulse of the *Zeitgeist*, the spirit of our age, he must soon have become aware of the occurrence and presence of a worldwide phenomenon which I have described and termed the " existential vacuum."

In fact, an ever-increasing number of patients approach a psychiatrist today complaining of a feeling of meaninglessness and emptiness. This existential vacuum seems to me to issue from the twofold fact that, unlike an animal, man is not told by drives and instincts what he *must* do; nor is he, like man in former times, told by traditions and values what he *should* do. Often he does not even know what he basically wishes to do.

Instead, he wishes to do what other people do — which is conformism. Or he does what other people wish him to do — which is totalitarianism.

Traditions are on the wane. But the crumbling of traditions only affects values, which are universal, and spares meanings, which are unique in that they change from person to person, and from situation to situation. Each life situation holds a unique meaning for every man. From this it follows that in an age such as ours, that is, in an age of the existential vacuum, education must not be satisfied merely with transmitting tradition and knowledge (in a reductionist manner at that as is often the case), but it must see its principal assignment in equipping man with the ability to find the unique meanings inherent in his unique life situations. This capacity is what is called conscience. In an age in which the Ten Commandments seem to many people to have lost their unconditional validity, man must learn carefully to listen to the *ten thousand* commandments involved in, and emerging from, the *ten thousand* unique situations of which his life forms a chain.

Thus conscience is a means to find meaning. And meaning must be found conscientiously — it cannot be given arbitrarily. For we are free not to invent meaning, but rather we are responsible for discovering it. In our democratic countries we enjoy our freedom, but perhaps we are not always fully aware of our responsibilities. Freedom, however, threatens to degenerate into mere arbitrariness or a form of anarchy unless it is experienced in terms of responsibleness. This is why I like to say that the Statue of Liberty on the Atlantic Coast should be matched by a Statue of Responsibility on the Pacific Coast.

Of course, we cannot tell a patient *what* the meaning of his life is; but we may well show him *that* there is a meaning to search for, to find out, and to fulfill. Even more than this, we may show him that the meaning of life remains, literally to his last breath. This is due to the fact that, as logotherapy teaches, even the tragic and negative aspects of life, such as unavoidable suffering, can be turned into human achievement by the attitude that a man adopts, by the stand that he takes toward his predicament. In contrast to most of the existentialist schools of thought, logotherapy is in no way pessimistic. It is just realistic in that it faces what I am used to calling the tragic triad of human existence: pain, guilt, and death. Indeed, logotherapy is even optimistic in that it also shows the individual how to take this challenge and how to transform his despair into a triumph.

What holds for any other psychiatric approach is also true of logotherapy. Logotherapy is not a panacea! However, in the age of the existential vacuum more patients than ever before may well be in need of the sort of psychotherapy that focuses upon " the search for meaning."

Viktor E. Frankl

Vienna, Austria

Contents

Preface

This book is about that frontierland of psychotherapy, religion, and the human self wherein extensive explorations are being conducted today. It is addressed to doctors of medicine, psychiatrists, ministers, and students who are concerned with new approaches in psychotherapy, their relevance to religion and the status of man in a technological culture. It was written in Vienna, itself a frontier of the West since it is situated less than a score of miles from the iron curtain of two totalitarian countries. Vienna once more draws the attention of the psychiatric world, for it is the home of Viktor E. Frankl, survivor of Nazi death camps and a founder of existential analysis.

By reason of the creative virtuosity and influence of its doctors, Vienna can be called the birthplace of modern methods in psychotherapy. Mesmer, founder of hypnotherapy, lived and practiced in Vienna in the eighteenth century before he was forced to leave the city. Feuchtersleben in the nineteenth century indicated in his writings a profound understanding of the intricacies of the human mind. The twentieth century saw the work of Freud, Stekel, and Adler, the founders of depth psychology. Of these, Freud and Adler organized schools of therapy, and today Frankl's trend in psychotherapeutic thinking is being called the third school to originate in Vienna.

Articles in American psychiatric journals a dozen years ago first called attention to Frankl's work. He had discovered that

7

certain neuroses responded to treatment only when problems centering about the meaning of existence were faced in therapy. His publications discussed the relevance of religion and psychotherapy, and he used the concept of *ärztliche Seelsorge*, " medical ministry," to describe what he felt was a responsibility of the doctor. In his thinking, medical psychology and pastoral psychology thus operate along a borderland of needs of the individual.

Pastoral psychology in turn did not originate in the recent flurry of interest in counseling. In the disciplines that theological schools call practical or pastoral theology, and theological anthropology, pastoral psychology reaches back through Augustine's candid confessions (of adolescent sexual and religious turmoil) to the very dawn of man's inquiries into his nature and destiny. Modern pastoral psychology as taught in the schools owes much to medical psychology, a fact most literature in the field recognizes.

Recently doctors and psychiatrists increasingly have become concerned over the role of pastors in counseling, for they meet each other on the doorstep of the sick soul. This concern over the extent to which the pastor is expected to give psychotherapeutic counseling is shared by theological teachers. They feel that deep problems in interpersonal relationships are not to be met by the pastor's assumption of the role of psychiatrist or his working as an amateur psychologist. Members of the medical profession today also are interested in what values religious insights may have to offer medicine and psychiatry. It is a familiar fact that to medical practitioners of all specialties come many patients who are not suffering from somatic illness. Does this indicate that the clergy have fallen down in mediating faith, hope, and love, or does it mean, as Frankl suggests, that doctors also must practice "medical ministry"?

Popular writings in psychotherapy and religion, when they are superficial, are a source of annoyance to both doctors and theologians, for they raise unreal expectations of the laity with hints of healing in three easy steps. However, a clearly recognizable trend points toward increasing co-operation between healing professions and enlightened religion. Medical schools and foundations are adding theological lecturers to their staffs, even as theological schools add more psychological training to their programs.

Discussion of psychotherapy and religion inevitably poses the question of the basic nature of man. This book suggests the necessity of facing this question seriously if psychotherapy is not to set itself up as a rival to religion, and if religion is to speak to the mind of modern man. Indeed, Prof. D. C. McClelland, of Harvard, argues that psychoanalysis already has many of the values of religion for those of the intelligentsia who enjoy its benefits, after having freed themselves from the enshackling bonds of more orthodox forms of religion. Dr. Farber, on the other hand, found that the theological insights of Martin Buber greatly benefited his psychiatric practice.

Whether a third school of Viennese psychotherapy will prove as influential as those of Freud and Adler can be settled only by history. That the insights of existential analysis have proved stimulatingly helpful is the opinion of many who have some acquaintance with Frankl's work. As this essentially is a report, I have attempted neither an exhaustive survey, nor a critical evaluation of strengths and weaknesses in the Vienna school of existential analysis. Frankl's work is still in the formative stage, still developing, and thus it is too early to sharpen the knives of dissection.

I am grateful to Professor Frankl for his wholehearted co-operation in making available all the resources of the Neurological Policlinic of Vienna for my year of study there on a Sealantic Fellowship. His suggestions and constructive criticisms during preparation of the manuscript enabled me to appreciate deeply the give-and-take encounter of persons in his school. Occasionally in the book there appear quotations from Dr. Frankl that are not documented with references. These are lecture items that were developed further in informal discussions and personal conversations with Dr. Frankl. Gratitude is expressed here for their encouragement and for manuscript correction patiently carried on by my wife, Mary, and daughter, Joan. Thanks are also due J. Benton Tulley and Herbert Booth Smith, Jr., whose long friendship I have often presumed upon for manuscript study. Their candid criticism from both lay and professional viewpoints has been deeply appreciated, as is that of several psychiatrist friends who made helpful suggestions. Jeannette Freeman deserves credit for producing exemplary typescript from my sometimes illegible writing.

A. J. U.

San Anselmo, California

Chapter I

Frankl's Existential Analysis

1. The Frontier Area

It is apparent today even to the most casual observer of Western culture that psychotherapy increasingly looms as an important rival of religion. Psychoanalysis may offer values of religious mysticism to its patients. Man's understanding of himself, of his existence, of his being, is a frontierland where both psychotherapy and religion are conducting extensive explorations. Neurosis can be described as man's progressive self-misunderstanding, and its familiar symptoms are anxiety, guilt, frustration, and boredom. Psychotherapy can be called a particular form of human relationship in which the therapist seeks to treat and heal neuroses and other disturbances that are emotional and mental in origin. In this relationship the patient or client is enabled to work out new and more satisfying patterns of living that help him to function more meaningfully in society. The aim is to help the patient to regain spontaneity, to achieve the courage and freedom to be himself, to be a self that he and others can respect.

Religion cannot be defined in a way that adequately covers either its history or its vast variety and range. The Christian religion, among others, in addition to its eternal reference emphasizing salvation, also has always had a vital interest in mundane affairs. It teaches that man works out his salvation in human relationships, that love and his capacity for love are essential ingredients of his religion. " He who does not love his

11

brother whom he has seen, cannot love God whom he has not seen." Religion also sees the suffering of man as an essential part of his existence, whether it is labeled neurotic or sinful. Both the psychotherapist and the pastor of religion agree that the freeing of man from guilt and anxiety is not an end in itself. The ultimate goal of both is to help suffering man realize his existence as one of deep, worth-while meaning.

Existential analysis is a fairly new form of psychotherapy that, having originated more or less spontaneously at several centers, has now come into considerable prominence in Europe. That it is bound to become influential in America is as certain as the fact that the tidal wave of Freudian psychology finally swept over America after decades of Freud's pioneer work in Vienna. Originating also in Vienna, the existential analysis of Viktor E. Frankl, himself a former student of Freud, will be the subject of my exploration. Like existential philosophy from which it draws insight and energy, existential analysis is focused upon the investigation of personal existence. Man's quest for being, for "the courage to be," his need for meaning in his existence, his uniqueness, subjectivity, freedom, and responsibility — all are used by the new therapy in healing the hurt of man.

Along with all psychotherapists, the existential analyst finds a prominent source of human suffering in the forefeiture of the self, or the flight of the self from the self. As one client said to me recently: "I find that I never have been a separate person. Always it seems I have tried to measure up to the demands of others, and only now am I beginning to be myself." Unlike some psychotherapy that shies away from philosophical entanglements as from anathema, existential analysis makes bold use of the contributions to our knowledge of the self, of human being, that are found in contemporary existentialism.

2. Biographical Notes

Prof. Viktor E. Frankl, of the medical faculty of the University of Vienna, long has been a student of existential philosophy, and as early as 1938 the term *Existenz-Analyse* was used in his writings. He possesses the doctorate in philosophy, as well as the medical degree, and is a practicing neurologist and psychiatrist, as well as Chief of the Neurological Polyclinic of Vienna. A vigorous man in middle life today, he had the unenviable opportunity of testing to the limits some of the theoretical propositions of existential philosophy when the Nazis confined him in a series of concentration camps including Auschwitz and Dachau during World War II. His description of his wartime experiences is found in his book *From Deathcamp to Existentialism.*[1] Here is a dispassionate account that plays down the horrors of life where men and women were subjected daily to brutal and meaningless sadism. Frankl's emphasis, however, is on what amounts to a crucial theme of existentialism: life involves suffering, and if life is meaningful, there must also be meaning in suffering, under any and all conditions. Yet in the camps Frankl, the doctor, could not tell his fellow sufferers what the purpose of it all was, and " prescribe " a meaning, for each man must find this out for himself. When all that makes life bearable and significant was deliberately removed, and the man himself enslaved, Frankl, the existentialist, could assert that there still remained freedom to choose attitudes toward this fate, attitudes that in many cases determined personal survival. What saved some men at least from despair was their appropriation of the existential truth of uniqueness, even though this existed on the slender margin of a unique opportunity to bear an appalling burden in a distinctive way.

At the outbreak of war, Frankl was a medical man of standing in the community, director of therapy in a large mental hospital. Working in the tradition of Adler's Individual Psychology, he had earlier organized a group of Youth Guidance Centers in the city of Vienna. These centers, staffed by psychiatrically trained doctors and counselors, offered guidance and help for young people in emotional difficulties. The success of this work in preventing suicide and in straightening tangled lives was so phenomenal that other cities organized their own centers after the Viennese pattern. During the Nazi regime in Austria, all psychiatry in the Freudian tradition was abandoned, and Freud himself barely escaped, seeking refuge in England.

As the calculated sadism of Nazi racial theory grew in severity and was put increasingly into practice, Viktor Frankl, along with many other doctors, was sent to a concentration camp. When first imprisoned, he attempted to take with him a complete manuscript, but this was confiscated and destroyed. His successful attempt to reconstitute the writing on scraps and bits of paper added to his purpose in living, and very likely enabled him to persevere. His entire family — wife, parents, and his brother with the exception of one sister living in Australia — perished in the concentration camps, all of this of course with no knowledge on his part until after the war ended, and he was liberated.

In one of his first public addresses after the war Professor Frankl testified as to the sustaining power of faith in a personal, living God, and he related the concept of collective guilt, which then was a popular device for settling responsibility for the war on certain nations, to the responsibility of man as individual man. At another memorial service for doctors who died in the camps he urged the abandonment of hate toward those who caused their death, and in place of hate he urged consideration of the existentialist concern of what it means to be — to be human! Today he lives quietly in Vienna with his second wife, Ellie, and his young daughter, Gabrielle, in a modest apartment located a few steps from the Polyclinic. His classes and clinical demonstrations in the ancient lecture hall of the Polyclinic create sustained interest among students, many of whom come from countries other than Austria.

A man of winsome personal charm, Frankl's modesty and capacity for tremendous exertion of energy remind one of genius. In fact, that is just what his distinguished colleagues consider him to be, and like a genius he is stimulating to work with in these creative bursts of energy. Relaxation from professional duties he finds in mountain-climbing, a sport in which he is quite adept, and in sketching cartoons and caricatures of his colleagues, a skill in which he is something of a master. As a teacher and doctor he never fails to put a patient at ease regardless of social status or education, and this in the presence of a large class at a clinical demonstration. Thus his existential theories of being are enacted in the concern of the therapist for the person and the needs of the patient.

The name *Existenzanalyse,* which Frankl has given to his school of therapy, has been translated into English as "Existential Analysis." For ontological reasons and to distinguish his approach from the existential analysis of Ludwig Binswanger, Frankl has also given the name "Logotherapy" to his system. Binswanger styles his work *Daseinsanalyse,* and in view of the difficulty in arriving at an exact English equivalent for *Dasein,* Binswanger's term is also translated as "Existential Analysis." The word *Dasein,* so important to existential thinkers among the Germans, means literally "there being," or "to be there," though translated as "presence," "existence," or "life." Interestingly enough, Marjorie Grene, a former student of Heidegger, translates it as "human being."[2] This may help make it easy to see why the words *Dasein* and "existence" carry with them a whole comet's tail of connotations that vary from philosopher to philosopher and therapist to therapist.

The *Daseinsanalyse* of Binswanger is not intended primarily as a therapy. More correctly, it is aimed at a better understanding of the psychoses and of the psychotic patient. The term *Dasein* as used by Binswanger[3] indicates a specific mode of being, namely, "human existence." His *Daseinsanalyse* therefore is particularly aimed at investigating the specific modes of "being in the world" — to quote the familiar phrase of Heidegger — as these are displayed in the various psychotic states. A member of the school, Medard Boss, has stated categorically: "*Die Daseinsanalyse hat nichts mit psychotherapeutischer Praxis zu tun.*"[4] ("Existential analysis has nothing to

do with psychotherapeutic practice.") Where the concept of
man as an existential person with several dimensions is involved in therapy, Frankl classified psychoanalysis as a dynamic, and Daseinsanalyse as a static, approach, in contrast
to his own existential analysis, which he calls an appellative
psychotherapy.[5] The word "appellative" refers to the methodology of his existential analysis. It appeals to other qualities
of man's being than just the depths of the unconscious processes, as for instance, man's authentic or primary concern with
meaning and value.

The existential analysis, or logotherapy, of Frankl is both an
analysis where this form of treatment is appropriate and also a
psychotherapy for the treatment of neuroses. Classic types of
neurotic illness, and also types of problems that are properly
nonneurotic in origin can be handled by this approach. Thus
where Binswanger's work is aimed at gaining a better understanding of the psychoses, Frankl's approach not only is focused on the treatment of neuroses but is also concerned with
the whole gamut of difficulties that the average psychotherapist of whatever orientation is called upon to face. Its insights
are applicable in psychiatry and psychoanalysis obviously, and
they offer valuable resources to clinical psychologists, counselors, educators, social workers, and pastors of religion who in
counseling and in the confessional deal with suffering man, or
Homo Patiens, as Frankl has entitled one of his books. This
term is also a basic tenet of logotherapy in that Frankl stresses
over and again that suffering belongs to human existence as an
essential element, so that suffering in itself is not considered by
him as something morbid, pathological, or neurotic. He insists,
for example, "that there are crises of inner growth, or of existential maturation, which are not at all to be identified with,
or traced back to, social maladjustment or lack of emotional
balance."

Interest in the new Vienna therapy is growing rapidly in
South America, and recently the Argentine Society for Existential Logotherapy decided to form two sections, one of which

includes nonmedical therapists who are thus acknowledged as sharing responsibility for treatment of mental and spiritual distress with the medical doctor. Frankl has said that "man's despair at not finding any meaning to his existence is in itself no disease; therefore, why hand him over to a psychiatrist? Such a case needs to be dealt with by a logotherapist, and not necessarily by a psychiatrist. Only those cases should be referred to the medical profession, in which one's existential concern over the meaning of his life has already led to neurotic complications in the strict sense of the term, or to what logotherapy calls noogenic neuroses." In the interests of clarification, the term "existential analysis," or "existential logotherapy," will be used henceforth in this book to indicate Frankl's school. References to the Binswanger school will be carefully qualified.

3. Existential Analysis as Logotherapy

The basic concepts of the logotherapeutic school of existential analysis are carefully defined. Though a mastery of their exact meaning is important for the psychotherapist, even more important is the attitude with which the therapist approaches the very being or existence of his patient. An analogy might be made between the strict rules for giving, scoring, and interpreting the Rorschach test, and the wide variance in practice among its users. I have seen a clinical psychologist spend two full days with a Rorschach and come up with a careful diagnosis that was later matched by the conclusions of a staff of medical men and psychiatrists. I have also seen a famous psychologist give, score, and interpret accurately the Rorschach in only a few minutes. Therapy often is a matter of many hours, but logotherapy offers promise that the years sometimes demanded by psychoanalysis can be cut down to weeks, if not hours, in certain cases. This is the impression I carried away from Vienna after a year of working with logotherapeutic methods in individual as well as in clinical and group therapy. Not only neurotics, but also psychotics, schizophrenic and paranoid patients, respond to both individual and group therapy.

Existential logotherapy aims at helping people who are troubled with doubts, despair, the meaning of life, and similar difficulties. These people may be seriously ill with somatic, or even psychotic, disturbances. They may also be people with no illness of body or mind, but still suffering from what is called in logotherapy *existential frustration* — despair over a meaningless life, and a lack of knowledge of what makes life worth living. *Existence* here too, as in the philosophy mentioned earlier, is the first concept that must be carefully defined and understood. It means, according to Frankl's usage, *being*, a certain kind of being, specifically and intrinsically human, which man, and man alone, is capable of attaining; " it is characterized by the ability of man to transcend himself, to emerge above himself, above the level of his own physical and psychic determinants, such as his heredity and his environment." [6] The being, man, can grapple with these determinants and shape them even as they seek to shape him, or he can supinely submit to them.

Man, therefore, does not merely exist, but rather, a portentous characteristic of his existence is precisely his personal influence upon successive stages of his existence. To paraphrase Jaspers, man continually decides what he is becoming, even as in ancient Judaism the solemn warnings and reiterations of the prophet helped bring into being the conditions for the fulfillment of his prophecy. Even the depressed and despairing person illustrates an important facet of this teaching about existence as special being: one whose failures and/or inferior feelings have given him a low estimate of himself " could not sit in judgment upon himself if he did not already possess the worth and dignity of a judge, of a man who has perceived what ought to be as against what at the moment is." [7]

The " ability of man to transcend himself " in the exercise and development of his being enables him to detach himself not only from himself (as in self-judgment or evaluation) but also from his world. Because he can do this, he can objectify or conceptualize the world, just as he can also objectify himself, encounter himself, or even oppose himself if necessary. Man is characterized by what Frankl calls "the human spirit's defiant power" (*die Trotzmacht des Geistes*); [8] he can defy the outer world, resist environmental forces as well as instinctual forces or drives. It is true, as psychoanalysis has convincingly urged, that man has instincts, but, as Frankl would also urge, these instincts do not necessarily have man! Nor, despite the marvelous "social" organization of bees and ants, do these creatures have the capacity of asserting themselves against instinctual or hereditary forces.

One of Frankl's disciples, Dr. Gertrude Paukner, adds a corollary at this juncture to remind us that man does not always need to oppose his instincts or heredity. Often he needs them for his purposes or goals, and therefore he is indebted to them. Mother love, for example, is an instinct that, of course, should not be opposed unless it smothers the child. That is why Frankl prefers to speak here of capacity and of necessity, or again, he mentions a "potential psychic-noetic antagonism" that can be actualized when necessary. Man is what he is, a human being, thanks to his heredity and his environment, but he can assert himself against conditioning factors. Only when he does so is he distinctly human, responsible for what he is becoming. He has, as an animal does, a latent hereditary disposition, and this particular facet of his total being includes gifts as well as limitations. But in contrast to the animal he remains responsible for the use he makes of these. The man whose heredity presents him with a set of facial features that suffer sadly in comparison with the classic profile of the movie hero has the choice of becoming embittered over his fate, of ignoring his looks, or of developing charm or wit at his own expense.

Readers who may remember O. O. McIntyre's syndicated newspaper column will recall his love for dogs and the many stories in which his anthropomorphism led him to attribute human capacities to his dogs. They occasionally were "naughty," "stealing" the cake, or tipping over a vase of flowers. The usual punishment was for the dog to be shut up in a closet, and occasionally McIntyre would come home to find the dog sitting in the closet. His interpretation was that the dog "felt guilty" and "knew" he would be punished. Though animal lovers have a right to their feelings, a dog cannot be "naughty," or steal, or feel guilty. These reactions are distinctly human, from the human dimension of life. Psychology, however, has clarified the many things men share with animals, and perhaps as Frankl intimates, "anticipatory anxiety" would more accurately describe the actions of our beloved four-legged friends! If guilt means anything at all, it certainly involves responsibility and freedom, two concepts with which some schools of therapy have failed to deal adequately.

Freedom and responsibility follow logically from the existential stress upon existence as the type of being that is continually emerging, that transcends the past in terms of present and future decisions. The patient or client is seen as a *being* to be understood as fully as possible, not as an object to be subjected to analysis and reshaped according to a preconceived set of postulates. The concept of man as *free* is a presupposition of existential analysis. Man has freedom: he is capable of real decisions, responsible acts. In his moving account of concentration camp life [9] Frankl details how a significant portion of freedom still was available to the inmates. Here were men who had been stripped of position, possessions, loved ones, everything, in a carefully calculated, sadistic determination to deprive them of pride, self-respect, and ultimately their life. Every day a man's personal number might be called to fill a quota for the gas chambers. Yet men still remained free under these appalling conditions to decide or choose what attitude they would take toward their treatment. Those who did not choose to use this marginal but real freedom gave up to despair or were themselves brutalized. Those who utilized their limited freedom to choose an attitude of hope found in it help to survive, achieved a degree of serenity that they were able to share with others, and even in their inescapable death they found meaning. The background here is no comfortable lecture-hall theorizing, but a rugged empiricism of camp life that put to the most extreme test the concept of freedom.

Freedom, however, is always associated with responsibility in Frankl's thought. Freedom too often means " freedom from something " in certain types of existential thinking, whereas *responsibility* is " to " or " for " something. Each person, each existent being, is responsible for attaining the utmost meaning that can be fulfilled in his life, in the course of which he is also responsible for realizing specific values. Here the general goal of self-realization as an aim of much psychotherapy and counseling has more specific directions laid before it. Here also is a careful qualification as to how the concept is to be used in therapy: " But the question of what man is responsible to cannot be answered in a general way, at least by ourselves as psychotherapists. For this question too has to be answered in a personal way, and we are not allowed to take the responsibility for answering it away from our patients. On the contrary, we have to educate them to the ability to shoulder their own responsibilities. We have to refrain from imposing our own world view on them." Frankl goes on to say that, among many answers to the question of responsibility, one can be responsible to another person, to society, conscience, or God. " This latter answer is given by the religious man who, as we see, actually does not feel responsible to some*thing* but to some*one*, to a personal, or better, to a suprapersonal entity." [10]

Karen Horney has written that "man, by his very nature, strives toward self-realization, and his set of values evolves from such striving." [11] Frankl adds to the findings of Horney his insistence that only to the degree to which man accomplishes certain specific tasks in the surrounding world will he fulfill himself. However, when Sartre speaks of man as " inventing himself," Frankl sharply denies this possibility and prefers to speak of " detecting " the self in its true dimensions, in its wholeness as man.

The concepts of existence, being, freedom, and responsibility bring us to the area of *values* and *meaning*, which are most significant in existential logotherapy. In the word " logotherapy" the Greek term *logos* is intended to signify the spiritual realm, or the noetic dimension of man. Due to the fact that the word "spiritual" (*geistig*, in German) has definite religious connotations in the English language, Frankl prefers, for therapeutic and ontological reasons, the use of the term "noetic." Logotherapy, like all psychotherapy, is primarily a secular discipline: it can be used by a doctor, psychologist, counselor, educator, pastor, and others. Logotherapy aims at restoring mental health, though its side effects, as Frankl shows in his book *Der Unbewusste Gott* (The Unconscious God) in some felicitous cases consist in a rebirth of the patient's religious life. The word "noetic," to repeat, is strictly a synonym for the word "spiritual" in its widest (German) meaning, but nevertheless, in its ontological use as well as in therapy, the door is left open to suprahuman dimensions. Logotherapy does not neglect man's spiritual needs, expectations, longings, and values, but then neither does it try to guide the religious development of the patient. In that dimension it defers, and when necessary, refers to the specialist in religion, the priest or minister. *Spiritual*, or *noetic*, then, refers to that class of psychic activity, specifically human, which is exemplified in moral decision; groping for meaning, option, or choice; responsibility; the ability to objectify oneself or oppose oneself; ability to conceptualize the world; the capacity of not being dependent upon instinctual drives, but the ability to sublimate them; the exercise of free will; the recognizing of, and deciding upon, values. By this definition Frankl avoids falling prey to any form of intellectualism or superrationalism, for he often emphasizes that the spiritual life of man is deeply rooted in the prerational, emotional sphere.

The second way in which the word *logos* was used when Frankl coined the term "logotherapy" signifies "the meaning," for this school stresses man's steady search for meaning as an inborne, innate, deeply rooted groping for an ultimate, higher meaning for his life. In much of its methodology the school sets out deliberately to evoke and to stimulate what Frankl has styled " the will to meaning," for it is man's most valuable asset. This insight is based upon facts, profound experiences, clinical and nonclinical evidence. The will to meaning is an asset not only in gaining or keeping mental health, in achieving happiness, or even in self-realization, but also it alone can enable man to realize the ultimate values and possibilities of which his life is capable. In the noetic dimension that man enters, he overcomes his animality. He remains an animal it is true, but now he is more than animal in his starting to realize existential values of being — just as an airplane moving along the ground does not cease to be an airplane but still does not fulfill its true destiny until it leaves the earth and is airborne.[12]

Experiences in the Nazi concentration camps gave Frankl vivid insight and firsthand knowledge of the validity of meaning and the necessity for values as they relate to man's existence. This necessity was evidenced among American Servicemen who were in prison camps in Japan and Korea. Dr. J. E. Nardini and other military psychiatrists were puzzled by the apathy of some men, which was so extreme that they died from no other apparent or diagnosed cause than lack of a will to live. Research established the fact that the men who gave up earliest, and with the least struggle, were those, usually the younger, who had had too little experience to establish meaning and values in life. The importance of this research was held to be so significant for military morale that tape recordings of its findings were made available to reserve units.[13]

By way of summarizing the chief emphasis in psychoanalysis Frankl styles it " the will to pleasure " in view of the pleasure principle of Freudian psychology. The Adlerian school of analysis is characterized by stress on the will to power. Logotherapy finds both operative in man's motivation, but even more significant is what Frankl calls man's " will to meaning." This becomes a clue for therapy in many of the difficulties that vex modern man. Maslow has pointed out that Freud's main mistake was in urging that *all* determinants of man's behavior are to be sought in the unconscious.[14] Many determinants are in

the unconscious, and as Freud rightly saw, they need to be de-
bunked, or unmasked as Freud called the process of making
them conscious, in order to find hidden motivation, wishes, and
instinctual drives. This admitted oversimplification is the essence of dynamic psychology. But there are other determinants
of behavior. In his latest book, *Das Menschenbild der Seelen-
heilkunde* (Stuttgart, 1959), Frankl bitterly criticizes so-called
unmasking psychology: here he states that "unmasking should
remain a means to an end, the primary end of making available
what is true in man!" If we understand him correctly, it follows that for psychoanalysis to take away delusions and self-
deceptions is a fine thing. But to continue the process to the
point of attempting to unmask what is *true* in man — his struggle for values, for meaning, and his spiritual strivings — indicates that "behind the tendency to debunk stands the hidden
tendency to depreciate spiritual values." Here the psychoanalyst may attempt to bend human nature to fit a preconceived
theory, instead of letting phenomenological evidence prod him
into re-examination of the theory.

An orthodox analyst, loyal to the Freudian categories, would
find it easy to "unmask" Frankl's will to meaning as a sublimation of instinctual drives, a defense mechanism, a secondary rationalization, or possibly a reaction formation. But to do
this is to run Freud's helpful insight and technique into the
ground, ostrichlike,[15] for fear of the necessity of examining new
evidence on human nature. Apropos here is an observation of
Dietrich von Hildebrand, a disciple of Max Scheler: "Finally,
the predominance of a psychological approach and the triumphant march of psychoanalysis also had their share in preparing
the dethronement of truth. The interest in psychological reasons why a person utters an opinion, affirms a thesis, holds a
position toward a theory, has replaced more and more the interest in the question of the truth of this opinion, this thesis or
theory — as soon as it [this approach] supplants the question of
the truth of the opinion, a disastrous perversion takes place."[16]

There are analysts who, having concluded a successful analysis, nevertheless feel that the treatment has failed and the patient has regressed if he returns to his religion after having been analyzed. If unmasking has brought to light an immature, magical religion, its God a celestial bellhop running errands in response to childish demands, or perhaps a buddy-pal, " the man upstairs " whose praises are sung with jukebox jingles, then psychoanalysis has done religion a real favor, and the pastor has no cause to become indignant. The responsibility can be placed squarely upon religious leaders with the question: Why do childish, unreal, un-Biblical expectations concerning God, life, suffering, death, persist in so many people to whom faith means assent to intellectual propositions and prayer either an unrecognized or a deliberate attempt to manipulate God? On the other hand, if unmasking reveals the striving of a mature adult for meaning and his need for transcendent reality as an anchor for life, can this existential " sorrowful concern " be recognized as a valid aspect of the human self, or is it to be rejected as illusory? If in answer to the first question above the pastor is to be held responsible for teaching religion as a mature, Biblical way of *living*, the psychoanalyst, who better than any man knows how much *unlived life* and how many crippling distortions of life exist, should hold himself responsible for a most serious concern with the nature and needs of the human self.

It could well be that Frankl's existential analysis will ultimately be recognized as pioneer work in calling psychoanalysis, and with it all psychotherapy, to the task of grappling with the issue of the nature of the human self. Years ago, however, another pioneer saw the implications that Frankl now seeks to make explicit. It is no longer generally known, even in analytic circles, that one of Freud's earliest American disciples was Dr. James J. Putnam, Harvard's professor of neuropathology when Freud visited America in 1909. Putnam, an enthusiastic convert to analysis, urged that it could be enriched by a fuller interpretation of human existence in terms of its freedom and basic nature. To him, the spiritual origin and transcendental reality of the self, along with ethics and the relevance of religion, were important aids for the interpretation of the knowledge of human dynamics through analysis that already was reaching impressive proportions. Freud, distrustful of metaphysics and religion, disagreed with Putnam as to the limits of naturalistic methodology for understanding man, and waived his suggestions politely but firmly aside, concluding thus: "It seemed more prudent to wait to discover whether a particular attitude toward life might be forced upon us with all the weight of necessity by analytic investigation." [17]

Psychoanalysis, and with it all forms of psychotherapy, is existential as well as scientific, and the pressures of modern life should force it to grapple with the formulation of a theory that is open to philosophical and also theological implications. Frankl in his existential analysis is aware that psychotherapy moves toward the frontier of religion, and that Christianity is concerned with the frontier of healing, for both are involved with the well-being of the whole human person. In logotherapy this well-being is sought by emphasizing meaning, but "when we speak of meaning, this is not intended in a general way but in a personal and concrete way, such as the attainment of vocational fulfillment, innermost wishes and values, a sense of personal mission which cannot be fulfilled by anyone else but only by one's own personality in a most exclusive and unique way. There is a life task awaiting everybody, which is to be actualized by himself alone. Existential logotherapy takes the will to meaning most seriously, for the primary concern of man is to invest as much meaning in life and to realize as many values as possible." [18] The existential depth of Frankl's thought can be seen in another contrast to the depth psychology, as well as being a corrective complement to it. The Freudian pleasure principle, obviously an instinctive and id-influenced concept, describes, I feel, the immature world view and needs of the small child who has little experience and understanding of a large and confusing world, but who does understand pleasure. The Adlerian insight into the important part played in the formation of neuroses by the sense of inferiority gives understanding of status drives, the need for superiority, and thus the power principle. This is a picture of the adolescent and of his world view, for his flexing of muscles and his aggressive tendencies often hide an anxiety lest he will not grow up to the full stature of a man. And now the picture as portrayed by logotherapy, that of the mature adult who gains the insight that life can be a process of infinite expansion, growth, or development: he sees the will to meaning as his guiding principle. Thus the development of the three schools of Viennese psychotherapy may be seen to mirror the ontogenetic development of the individual from childhood to maturity.

Logotherapy tackles the ancient body-mind problem by casting it into a new and fresh approach that was termed by Frankl "dimensional ontology." Rejecting an older way of viewing man in several levels or layers of being, Frankl speaks of dimensions, distinguishing among them, the somatic, psychic, and the spiritual or noetic. These exist in heuristic contrast to one another, but this does not mean that man is "composed" of "body, mind, and soul." Unity and wholeness are affirmed without ignoring the differences between soma, psyche, and spirit. This ontology provides a method of recovering the wholeness and unity of man that seem to be endangered by tendencies in the social sciences to manipulate man as an object. A favorite illustration of Frankl's is the projection of a drinking glass onto a two-dimensional plane. From one projection comes the image of a circle, and from the second, a rectangle. Just as one would not urge that a glass is composed of a circle and a rectangle, Frankl urges that man cannot be viewed as composed of different layers. Gestalt psychology has taught us that the whole (of a musical chord, for example) is more than the mere sum of its parts. Man, too, in logotherapeutic conceptualization is more than the total sum of physical structure, reflexes, emotions, drives, and mental processes. Dimensional ontology offers a way of preserving the unity and wholeness of man, with all its undeniable and insurmountable differences between the dimensions fully recognized in their mystery.

"In the frame of reference of neurology, for example, man

necessarily appears as 'nothing but' a 'closed' system without any place left for something like a soul. We must be aware of the self-deception that this dimension of neurology is the only one which exists. As long as I have to examine a patient neurologically I have to 'behave as if' he existed only in this dimension. But when I put my reflex hammer aside, I broaden my view again. I encounter him as man to man, I to thou. I follow him into the fullness of dimensions, and into the wholeness of a human being, and this means of a somato-psycho-spiritual being, who again will become perceptible. Science is compelled to limit its view, to disregard the fullness of phenomena it has to deal with and to ignore those dimensions with which it has not to deal. But the scientist himself must know what he is doing. He must know that he is doing 'as if,' and this means that his work is, to a certain extent, based upon the indispensable fiction of an unidimensional reality." [19]

A final definition of what is meant by "values" in logotherapy must now be made before discussing its technique or methodology. As a therapeutical method, existential logotherapy seeks to help the patient find the utmost meaning in his existence. It does this by enabling him not only to see the possibilities of values but also to discover their relevance for his own personal life. According to logotherapeutic teachings, there are three kinds: *creative* values, *experiential* values, and *attitudinal* values. The first two kinds are familiar in the thinking and experience of many people. It is in the third group, attitudinal values, that Frankl has made a profound and unique contribution to psychotherapy of all orientations. It is a deep philosophical insight that emerged unshaken from the man-made hell of the concentration camp, and has since been tested in the Vienna clinic in the neurotic and schizophrenic hell of mental and emotional illness. Here is an insight that transcends the profoundest of Freud's contributions. It has proved itself adequate to meet the deepest needs of man, whether these rise in the objective results of inhumanity that led Wordsworth to mourn "what man has made of man," [20] or within the subjective agonies of spiritual (noetic) turmoil that Frankl has called existential frustration.

Creative values are those which result from acts and accomplishments that add to the world's knowledge and beauty or to the welfare of mankind. Many people arbitrarily limit creativity to the highly accomplished, assuming that since they cannot paint a great picture or compose a symphony, they cannot be creative. Contradicting this type of defeatism, the adult education movement has uncovered an appreciation of, and capacity for, creative work unsuspected by many. Grandma Moses, who attained fame as a painter in her eighth decade, is a cheerful example here. Vocational counseling can make fruitful application of the challenge of creative values in the light of the vocational unhappiness of many people. "The crucial thing is how . . . [a man] works, whether he fills the place in which he has landed. The radius of his activity is not important; important alone is whether he fills the circle of his task." [21]

Experiential values in turn are realized when one becomes sensitive or receptive to truth or beauty, whether in nature or in art. The capacity of natural beauty, of great music, or of stimulating truth to arouse responsiveness in the human spirit results in experiential values that add meaning to life. The third of the philosophical triad, goodness, needs also to be mentioned, for the utter kindliness of certain genuinely mature persons has a therapeutic value in the lives of those whom they influence. According to Frankl, "to know just one single human being in all his uniqueness is to experience mature love." Again: "The fullness of meaning which such values bring to human life must not be underestimated. The higher meaning of a given moment in human existence can be fulfilled by the mere intensity with which it is experienced, and independent of any action. For even though only a single moment, is in question, the greatness of a life can be measured by the greatness of a moment, and a single moment can retroactively flood an entire life with meaning. Let us ask a mountain climber who has be-

held the alpine sunset and is so moved by the splendor of nature that he feels cold shudders running down his spine — let
us ask him whether after such an experience his life can ever
again seem wholly meaningless." [22] Frankl, the artist, also
speaks as one whose favorite hobby is mountain-climbing.

It is in the third range of values that we meet the full therapeutical impact of this phase of existential logotherapy. *Attitudinal values* are to be achieved precisely in the arena of the
limiting factors upon one's life. Here the philosophical insight
can become a precision tool of great therapeutic power in the
hands of the skilled analyst, psychiatrist, or counselor. Where a
life has been strictly limited as to creative and experiential values, it still can be led in therapy to achieve greatness in its attitudes. I must mention the fact that these value categories do
not preclude the necessity of attitudinal values for the gifted
person as well as for limited people. The Vienna clinic records
tell of many persons, rich in creative and in experiential values,
who still came with deep neurotic illness that was cured by the
therapy of attitudinal values. But here it is the *ärztliche Seel-
sorger,* " the medical minister," in Frankl that leads him to put
his main emphasis on the problem of human suffering. His wartime experiences as well as clinical work have given him a deep
understanding and appreciation of the depths and the heights
of every conceivable type of human suffering.

Creative and experiential values, particularly when the experience of mature love is a component, all go to make life
meaningful. Existential logotherapy is ready to meet man,
however, when creativity fails to give values to life and experience no longer gives meaning to it. A man can still find
life purposive, and can demonstrate this by the way or manner
in which he faces the inevitable or the way in which he handles
suffering; here, Frankl teaches, is a last chance to realize values
and he quotes Goethe: " There is no condition which cannot
be ennobled either by a deed or by suffering." *Mere suffering,*
however, we humans share with the animal world. Logotherapy
urges that it is the right kind of suffering, the way in which it is

accepted, the attitudes we display toward our necessary burden, that enable us to realize the highest and finest kind of meaning for our life. " Thus, life has meaning to the last breath. For the possibility of realizing attitudinal values — by the very attitude with which we face our suffering — is there to the last moment." Logotherapy therefore gives suffering the status of a positive value.

In evaluating the attitudinal teaching of logotherapy, Dr. Edith Weisskopf-Joelson, a psychiatrist and professor on the staff of Purdue University, has said: " Such a value system may help counteract certain trends in our present-day civilization where the incurable sufferer is given very little opportunity to be proud of his unavoidable and inescapable suffering, and to consider it ennobling rather than degrading." In another context she writes: " Our current mental hygiene philosophy stresses the idea that people ought to be happy, that unhappiness is a symptom of maladjustment. Such a value system might be responsible for the fact that the burden of unavoidable unhappiness is increased by unhappiness about being unhappy." [23] Frankl holds that happiness is not goal enough for therapy, since it is a side effect of other more significant purposive action. Dr. Joelson continues: " Happiness is not explicitly considered a by-product of the attainment of other values. People can attain happiness more easily when they don't strive for it intentionally." [24] It follows that a deep, inner serenity can actually be a concomitant of suffering, and without a trace of morbidity because of the right attitude of the victim of suffering.

Recently a physician wrote in a popular journal to complain that people no longer are allowed to die in dignity. He felt that often there is too much medical interference at the last, with the patient doped into unconsciousness and his family hurried into the corridor of the hospital. This is of course a medical, religious, and social or family problem, but in this discussion I have quoted a general practitioner, a psychiatrist, and a neurologist, all of whom urge a more mature attitude toward suffering and death, for death, as Frankl says, is as much a part of life as anything else. My own personal life has been enriched by the attitudes three close friends developed as they faced slow death by incurable disease. In attempting to understand their strength, it came to me one day that its meaning lay precisely in the fact that they were triumphant, as *men,* over their illness long before that illness was victorious over their bodies! An aunt with an inoperable cancer, but also with an incurable sense of humor, wrote me that people came from all over Indiana to comfort her in her last days. "But several times," she wrote, "the room was filled with mournful and weeping people whom *I* had to cheer up!" In such an attitudinal triumph there lie the seeds of an argument for immortality if one needs the bolstering of argument. Just how the doctor goes about helping the patient achieve attitudinal values will be discussed next.

4. The Technique of Logotherapy

The basic therapeutic approach of logotherapy depends upon man's freedom to change his attitudes. It therefore seeks to stimulate the patient to change his attitudes toward his difficulties or his neurotic symptoms. This is a conscious process, and it must be said in this connection that logotherapy, well aware of the importance of the psychogenesis of neurosis in the affect-dynamics, feels that the treatment of the spiritual distresses of man, such as despair and the feeling of meaninglessness, is still more important. It is a fine thing to trace present difficulties back to their source, as in the relatively simple analytic procedure of helping a man who has perennial difficulties with his employers to see that his unconscious feelings of aggression toward his long-dead father are a major cause. But if in addition to poor employer relations he finds his work an empty thing because his life appears futile, the methods of conventional psychotherapy if it is wary of philosophical involvement do not apply. If the world view of the patient is involved, this is an intellectual problem, often hidden by neurotic symptoms, and this calls for a psychotherapy in terms of the mind. Many a therapist in conventional psychotherapy has helped his clients with such problems, for as Frankl says of logotherapy: "*De facto* its aims are not new and its approach has been tried, usually unwittingly. However, we are here examining the possibility of applying logotherapy *de jure*, and striving to determine in which cases and to what extent it is desirable." [25]

After a paper delivered by Frankl on the invitation of the San Francisco Theological Seminary at San Anselmo, Dr. Sutherland, one of the psychiatrists present at the seminar, remarked that he had been unconsciously a logotherapist all the time. In his concluding remarks Frankl replied that he himself was convinced that "every good doctor always has performed logotherapy without necessarily knowing it. But if logotherapy would have nothing more to offer than making conscious and methodological what has been previously a result of individual intuition and improvisation, this in itself would be a worth-while achievement, for by this very fact it would have become teachable and learnable."

Existential logotherapy, as a special form of psychotherapy, is not intended to replace it, but to supplement its tested methods with a special approach for special problems. As one of its tasks logotherapy proposes to handle philosophical problems within their own frame of reference. Without denying the truth in the psychoanalytic theory and method of handling the *irrational* influences of the unconscious, existential logotherapy does not propose to slough off the responsibility of handling *rational* problems in a rational way. Human beings suffer not only from irrational fears and anxieties but also from psychic disturbances that have intellectual causes, and these respond to objective discussion. Frankl has clarified this differentiation in the following statement: "A doctor must carefully distinguish between psychic disease and spiritual distress; otherwise he might run the danger of suffocating the man's despair over a seemingly meaningless existence by prescribing tranquilizers."

This is no narrow school with a strict credo or party line. Frankl would invite all psychotherapists to become fellow workers in logotherapy. In fact, since Jung early in the twentieth century defined neurosis as "the suffering of a soul that has not found its meaning," we could call Jung the first logotherapist! The suffering soul is the first consideration of existential logotherapy; the warped mind, entangled in hate and failure to love, may respond to conventional therapy, and then again it too may need "logos."

The student looking for a systematized procedure of techniques in logotherapy will see that what is here emphasized is not a set of prescribed techniques, but rather the improvisation, inventing, and individualizing of techniques, adapting them to each individual case. Rigid categories are not offered into which the patient must be fitted or expected to conform. The patient and his illness or the client and his problems may seem very similar to others in the casebooks, but he is to be treated with respect to his individual uniqueness in relation to all other patients. Frankl holds that too great an emphasis upon technique produces technicians, not therapists, and then the patient becomes a machine to be manipulated in accordance with prescribed techniques. When he speaks of medical ministry, where the doctor introduces philosophical questions, when these are relevant, into medical practice, he frankly admits that it is not therapy, as such, at all. For "in such cases it is not the disease which is being dealt with (or even cured), but rather, the patient's attitude toward his illness which then has to be changed." Even medicine and surgery cannot very often separate symptoms and illness from anxieties, attitudes, meaning, and responsibility. These are usually entangled in the patient's life, and they tend to entangle the therapist too when he enacts his acceptance. If we remember that logotherapy sees the basis of human existence in the consciousness of responsibility and the attainment of meaning, its technique hinges upon methods of bringing about that consciousness.

An open avowal of the clinical significance of meaning and

of values is central in the logotherapeutic approach to the difficulties of the patient. Existential logotherapy teaches that man's feeling of the meaninglessness of life, the condition that Frankl calls existential frustration, may also produce a certain type of neurosis. This neurosis obviously does not, as in many other neuroses, have its source in various complexes or traumata extending as far back perhaps as infancy. It arises from intellectual problems, moral concerns, spiritual or ethical conflicts. This nonphysiological and nonpsychological neurosis Frankl has called " noogenic," and it requires the appropriate therapy. This is " logos-therapy, which is a therapy oriented toward meaning, and it involves reorienting the patient toward meaning." [26] In order to attain meaning for his life and to find values for that life, the patient has to accept responsibility. Logotherapy specifically aims at stimulating the patient's capacity for responsibility. Upon the assumption or recognition of responsibility the patient proceeds *independently* to the problem of existential meaning as it touches specifically his own life, needs, and potentialities. In this task he is aided by the therapist who points out the possibility and necessity of choosing a way, and the direction to travel on that way; but the traveler must make his *own* choice, for he travels alone.

Counselors will readily see in this aspect of logotherapy certain similarities to Professor Rogers' client-centered therapy. Like Rogers, Frankl insists: " First of all there must be no imposition of the personal philosophy of the doctor, of his personal concept of values, on the patient. The logotherapist must be careful to see that the patient does not shift his responsibility onto the doctor." [27] The student of Rogers' method sometimes forgets the importance of what Rogers means by clarification of responses and the communication of understanding to the client. In his eagerness to deal correctly with the problem of responsibility just mentioned, he falls into the error of " mirror responses " that indicate lack of empathy and rapport. Frankl's approach differs from client-centered counseling in having, perhaps, a more explicit relationship to a philosophical world view [28] and in recognizing responsibility, meaning, and values as clinical means of overcoming neuroses. In his paper read at the World Congress for Psychotherapy at Barcelona, in 1958, Frankl said: "It is not logotherapy's concern that we therapists *give* the patient a meaning for his existence, but only that we *enable* him to find such a meaning, that we, so to speak, broaden his field of vision so that he will become aware of the full spectrum of the possibilities for personal and concrete meaning and values."

The medical background of existential logotherapy reminds us that the function of the doctor, from the days of Hippocrates, is to console where he cannot heal. The philosophy of the old family doctor used to be: "Heal a few, treat many, comfort all." The modern doctor, so successful in curing so many diseases formerly incurable or fatal, finds an increasingly large number of his patients with psychogenic complaints. Where these are tied up with, or due to, what Frankl calls "existential vacuum," or existential frustration, logotherapy offers the appropriate treatment.

The classification of neuroses as they are dealt with in logotherapy is as follows: (1) Psychogenic neuroses — those arising from psychic conflicts. Here logotherapy often operates on the same level as conventional psychotherapy. (2) Somatogenic, or "pseudoneuroses" — those arising from vegetative and endocrine disorders. (3) Noogenic [29] neuroses, those which do not stem from any complexes or traumata but which result from spiritual problems or moral conflicts. Frankl urges that the proper place to look for causes of this type of sickness and the proper place to begin its treatment is not in "depth conflicts," but precisely in the sphere of the noetic where the sickness originates. (4) Existential frustration, which does not involve a condition of psychic illness but rather a condition of spiritual distress. The existence of such a condition definitely is not pathological or symptomatic of mental disease. According to Frankl, "It is something human, even the most human of all there may be in man."

A definite technique of logotherapy that Frankl has called "paradoxical intention" has drawn attention and interest. It consists in urging the patient to quit fighting his symptoms, and paradoxically, to exaggerate them to a humorously ridiculous extreme. This idea is based upon the fact that the more a patient tries to fight his neurotic symptoms, the more intensely these symptoms manifest themselves. The amusing story of Immanuel Kant and his dishonest servant points this up. Having discharged the man for dishonesty, Kant mourned his absence, but his ethics forbade him to miss him so much. So he put a large sign above his desk to remind him: "Lampe must be forgotten." Of course as long as the sign remained he could not forget his servant. The neurotic similarly gets into a solipsistic circle of fighting his symptoms, which are thereby intensified. In paradoxical intention, a patient who has neurotic fears of heart attacks is urged to "talk to" his symptom thus: "Well, I must go out on the street and have a heart attack. Yesterday I had two attacks; let's better the record today and make it three!" The patient of course smiles at the ridiculousness of this, but if he puts paradoxical intention into effect, he is enabled to make full use of his sense of humor and overcome his neurotic fears.

To go a bit deeper into what will occur to many therapists of other schools as a superficial if not dangerous technique: This approach is based upon the specifically human ability to detach one from oneself, or to oppose oneself in the sense of transcendence as that concept is used in existential philosophy. The ability to detach oneself from neurotic symptoms purposely calls upon a sense of humor. Allport states that "the neurotic who learns to laugh at himself may be on the way to self-management, perhaps to cure."[30] A patient troubled by obsessive suicidal thoughts may be asked by Frankl: "Why don't you commit suicide?" One such patient, who had been treated twenty years ago with the device of paradoxical intention, came back recently to pay the clinic a visit. He reported that he had been completely free of his obsessive suicidal thoughts after a few interviews. Before therapy he had been haunted for years by the fear of going mad and hanging himself. "What did I recommend to you?" asked Frankl. "Oh," replied the man, "you advised me to buy a rope and carry it continually in my pocket, and whenever the fear of suicide occurred to my mind, you told me I should say to myself: ' Let's now go and hang myself; here is the rope all ready.' At that moment I had to laugh, and from that time on the obsession gradually disappeared."

It must be pointed out here that paradoxical intention as just described was used by a neurologist and psychiatrist, skilled in diagnosis. The average counselor would be ill advised to assume the method to be a "universal antiseptic" for all suicidal patients. That such a misinterpretation could cause a lot of damage is an obvious understatement. The ability to distinguish between psychotic and neurotic symptoms, between real and pseudoneuroses requires psychiatric and diagnostic skill, clinical experience and intuition as well. Above all it must be said that paradoxical intention may be successfully applied in cases of suicidal obsession like that mentioned above, but never in a case of true suicidal impulse as it is met with in endogenous depression; here the method would endanger the patient, for it would encourage him to destroy himself.

Paradoxical intention, however, can be used in less dramatic or urgent cases than that of the would-be suicide. A theological student once became fed up with formal religious training and decided that God and the church were no answer to the pressing problems of humanity. His teachers urged him to stay with his studies until he got a grip upon them and upon himself, but as his counselor I agreed that the church was a mess, that God might not be the answer, and urged him to follow his inclination to do social work in a large city. There he organized community life, built a large social center, and was beloved by the people. But after two years he reported back to his theological school. "The work went fine," he explained, "but then people wanted to be married, buried, baptized, and instructed in religion. They asked questions of meaning that drove me back to school." Today he is a strong and respected leader in his church. The paradoxical counsel to shelve God and the church enabled him to attain the necessary objective standpoint from which to review his own scale of values and meaning.

A clinical case of the success of paradoxical intention can also be reported here from the records of the Vienna Polyclinic. Recently a woman, aged sixty-five, was admitted in order to have a leucotomy (brain surgery) performed that was deemed the only and final hope of bringing her relief. For sixty years, dating from the age of five, she had suffered from an extreme form of neurosis, with compulsions of washing and toilette preparation, due to an abnormal fear of bacteria. Everyone familiar with Freud's teaching on the oral, anal, and genital stages of development, together with the insights developmental psychology has gained therefrom — the effects of too-rigid training by parents and various other possibilities of serious traumata — could probably write a reasonably correct diagnosis of the *cause* of this unfortunate woman's difficulty. Yet even the most enthusiastic of orthodox analysts is not very sanguine over possible results of analysis with a case of such long duration.

Before surgery was carried out in this case, Frankl's associate, Dr. Eva Niebauer, of the Neurological Polyclinic, decided no harm could come from trying paradoxical intention. She recommended to the patient to " try again and again to do what she had been afraid of all this time, namely, to come into contact with bacteria. Within a few days the patient really succeeded in the intention of plunging into bacteria, as it were, to wash her hands in bacteria." Eventually the woman was washing basins and gradually did more work that exposed her precisely to the thing of which she was most afraid and which had so restricted her whole life. She assisted in the general ward work, which involved cleansing the hospital basins and vessels. Dr. Frankl himself was astounded at the results and canceled the plan for surgery. Within a few weeks the compulsive neurosis was so reduced that only supportive therapy was needed, and today the woman leads a normal life.

A character neurosis is greatly affected by the attitude adopted by the patient toward his own character structure. A fearful patient is confronted by fears of all kinds: he may fear that he is going to become psychotic, or that he may kill someone. By fighting these ideas they often merely become stronger. In these clinical cases the therapist, using paradoxical intention, may prompt the patient to tell himself: " Let's pick up the knife and go out to kill someone. Yesterday I killed several, today I will kill even more! " The very effrontery of the suggestion first startles the patient, and then it makes him smile. This *puts distance* between himself and the haunting obsessions, and thus he is better enabled to handle such thoughts. The primary purpose is to stop the fight against the obsessive ideas by encouraging the patient to exaggerate those ideas. As is seen in the case of the sixty-five-year-old patient, this can lend itself to short-term therapy. For deeper neuroses it obviously should be confined to practice in a clinical setting.

Existential logotherapy, as I have tried to make clear, not only enters the area of meaning, responsibility, and values, which in itself is enough to make the pure scientist's statistical hair stand up on end, but it also leaves the noetic door wide open for the invasion of religious values into man's life. Freud is the recognized scholar of the unconscious, and from its depths he has dragged enough to make more honest men out of all of us. I have no desire to belabor his view of religion as an illusion here, other than to suggest the possibility that it is not a true conclusion of depth studies. It would appear to be more of a rationalization that summarized the failure of Victorian culture and religion to solve the existential boredom of his neurotic patients. On the other hand, it is quite obvious that God is a father projection of the many immature folk to whom he is a celestial Santa Claus, whose praises they sing with jukebox music. Everything that Freud has done to expose this type of emotional fantasy is a service for religion.

After more research, depth studies someday may be able to explain a bit better *why* men are driven to project a father image, or why men everywhere try to make gods in their own image. Admittedly, the unconscious contains material that is so "awe-full" that we cannot face it, and that is why it has been repressed. Is it not also possible that the unconscious contains also that which is so awesome in its reminder of a complete goodness or holy "otherness" that here too we cannot stand the comparison it demonstrates with our imperfection? Hence, we thrust it, too, deeply out of sight, and come up with lesser gods like the divine daddy in the sky, or maybe "duty" or "energy." The father-image idea is much older than Freud. Psychoanalysis gives us a view of the reverse image of the ancient truth that reads: man is made in the image of God. If the dynamic psychology is truly dynamic, it must be seen that the unconscious becomes a repository of positive as well as negative factors of experience. Then religious convictions that have been repressed could issue forth as hostility toward religion, and this in part may account for the judgment that it is an illusion.

The religious views of Freud, Jung, and Fromm have received widespread hearing. It is to be hoped that a similar attention will be given to the religious concerns of an existential analyst such as Frankl. Many of these are recorded in his book *Der Unbewusste Gott* (The Unconscious God), which has been translated into several other languages and now is scheduled for translation into English. As its title indicates, it is a provocative reminder that the last word has not yet been written on God, man, and the unconscious.

Analytic procedure, so fruitful in giving us a deeper understanding of many aspects of human nature, still leaves other areas of human nature unexplored, as evidenced by the many variations in its own theory and practice. Its early practitioners, ebullient with the success that always follows stimulating innovation, can be forgiven their enthusiasm in urging that here was the solution to knotty problems that have vexed the seers and priests of all ages of man. Alexander the Great, it is recorded, also once cut a knot, but was not his motivation the "power drive" of immature impatience? Religion in the twentieth century with its pastoral counseling and education has gained a great deal from psychology and psychoanalysis, as many books in these fields demonstrate. And as to religion itself, its real truths and insights were not the result of dogmatic assertions of ecclesiastical councils, as the uninformed skeptic sometimes assumes, but they were wrested from human experience as men struggled for meaningful existence and found it. Perhaps these insights in turn can help psychology to gain further knowledge of human nature.

The leading logotherapists of various countries, undaunted by charges that "dabbling" in philosophy and religion has no place in therapy, continue to find therapeutic power in philosophical values, in the open-door policy toward religion. The approach is effective in the clinic, in counseling, group therapy, and in outpatient work. Some of the limitations of conventional psychotherapy can be met by the methods of logotherapy. But logotherapy too has its limitations, and passes over into what Frankl has called "medical ministry," and when limitations are reached here, religion is the next province. The area that existential analysis or logotherapy enters is, after all, a borderline country. "Medical ministry operates along a great divide – the dividing line between two countries must remember that he is under surveillance from two sides." [31] When a surgeon completes a successful amputation, he takes off his gown, but has he completed his duty? "Of what use has the surgical therapy been," asks Frankl, "if the patient then commits suicide because he cannot bear living as a cripple?" Not only the counselor and psychiatrist but also the physician can benefit from exploring the meaningful values that can be attained in one's attitudes toward inescapable suffering and limitations. Gordon Allport has given an excellent summary of this problem in his introduction to Frankl's report on the concentration camps.

All psychotherapy aims at helping people to mental and physical health, to work, to "adjust" and to enjoy life. Logotherapy includes these aims within its scope and goes on realistically to teach that there also is in man a capacity to suffer, not in a morbid, self-pitying way, but in a dignified, proud, self-realizing way. "Thus death does not cancel out the meaning of life, for it belongs to life as the end does to a story. Having been," urges Frankl, "is also a kind of being, perhaps the surest kind. The average man often sees just the stubble fields of transitoriness, and he overlooks the full granaries harvested from the past." The facts of a meaningful existence wherein one has accepted his responsibilities thus are unassailable by death. To achieve this kind of meaning in the necessary day by day decisions, Frankl offers this maxim of existential analysis: "Live as if you were living a second time, and as though you had acted as wrongly the first time as you are about to act now!" This maxim utilizes Frankl's central teaching that man behaves not only according to *what he is,* but according to what he is deciding to be. Man is continually shaping and deciding his essential self. He is not hewn out of stone upon which the traumata of experience leave eternally disfiguring marks.

Psychotherapy inevitably will have to face the problem of the self, and here a remark of Frankl's is apropos. "Man could be defined as the being who invented gas chambers for human extermination. But man can also be defined as the being who entered those gas chambers with the stirring tune of the 'Marseillaise,' or the Lord's Prayer, on his lips!" This would remind the historian of ancient Rome when, during a persecution of the church, the leader Tertullian found himself one day before a Roman judge who was exasperated by his calm spirit. "Do you not know that I have the power to kill you?" demanded the judge. "Yes," came the reply, "but I have the power to be killed!" Here was a situation that the existential analyst would call an attitudinal triumph.

Chapter II

Theory and Therapy

1. The Impact of Existential Philosophy

Existential analysis, though critical of some aspects of psychoanalysis, is not in reaction to Freud's great contributions. The new analysis can be described more accurately as a complementary therapy that builds upon those Freudian foundations which have stood the test of time and therapeutic practice in various schools. The structure being reared promises, however, to be somewhat different from the orthodox and more deterministic architecture of the past. Frankl concedes that Freudian psychoanalysis certainly will remain a lasting basis of psychotherapy; but he reminds us that it will have to share the fate of each kind of foundation, which is to become proportionately invisible as the building is erected. With characteristic humor he compares himself to Freud in terms of the allusion to a dwarf standing on the shoulders of a giant, and then adds with a smile, " Of course the dwarf can see farther than the giant."

What is challengingly new and stimulating in the new analysis is the application of the relevant insights of existential thinking to psychotherapy. The list of writers being labeled " existential " grows longer with every new publication that dips into the history of the movement. Though Kierkegaard is generally recognized as having detonated the bomb presently affecting us with its fallout, Descartes and Pascal did significant research that set the stage for his work. Pascal particularly is deserving of the attention of those interested in tracing the development of the existential approach to human nature and its problems.

An unquestioned leader of contemporary existential philosophy is Martin Heidegger. Hard to read, and difficult to understand, even his detractors and foes reluctantly admit his central position of influence in the modern scene. To his writings not only the Continental psychiatrists but also theologians have paid close heed. Though it is said Barth prefers not to admit the connection, both his theology and Bultmann's demythologizing approach to New Testament research show the influence of Heidegger's philosophy. In America the works of Reinhold Niebuhr and Paul Tillich indicate a thorough familiarity with Heidegger's existentialism.

Another name one finds frequently in publications of the existential psychotherapists is that of Karl Jaspers. He is both a psychiatrist and a professor of philosophy. Already in the second decade of this century his writings were exposing the mechanization of man, the depersonalization that has accompanied the growth of technological science. Mass production, Jaspers holds, has tended to produce mass man, mediocre, stereotyped, or as recently styled, "the organization man." A name well known in America, due to publicity created by some of his disciples, is that of Jean-Paul Sartre, an ardent admirer of Heidegger. It is said that Heidegger does not return the admiration, and an apocryphal version has him saying, "My God, I did not intend *that!*" Many Germans tend to consider Sartre primarily as a playwright and literary man rather than as an existential philosopher. Others see him as a legitimate member of the flock, despite the color of his wool.

Sartre's public relations have suffered from the fact that the "beat" generation of Paris and the Beatniks of San Francisco have pounced upon some of his views to supply a rationale for their neo-Bohemian style of studied purposelessness in living. His literary genius in addition to his experience in the French *maquis* of World War II give him a peculiar authority that deserves a respectful hearing. Henri Peyre describes Sartre's writings on the sad, vicious, nauseating aspects of life as an "inverted mystical experience." I feel it is possible that Sartre may yet dig his pit so deep that from its bottom, even in the daylight, he too may view the stars. The way of denial, and the results of the *via negationis* have surprised more than one mystic, both before and since Paul's trip to Damascus.

It is not feasible here to discuss all philosophers and existential writers who have influenced the existential psychotherapy that is still being developed in Europe and elsewhere. Two more names require mention, however: Max Scheler, whose writings and critiques are held in high regard by the Vienna school of existential logotherapy, and Sören Kierkegaard, who died more than a century ago. The latter originated a great deal of the terminology of existentialism and he remains a definite source spring of modern work in the field. Existentialism already includes such a variety of valiants and camp followers that Kierkegaard never would acknowledge all of them as his literary or philosophical descendants. Those acquainted with his life will agree that his reaction would be more explosive than that of Heidegger if the matter of paternity were broached! The capacity of a philosophy to stimulate in diverse directions is seen in the contrast between the work of Karl Barth, who applies what is relevant in existential thought to a profound theological system, and the writings of Sartre, who works in a naturalistic milieu. The contributions of Tillich could be similarly contrasted with those of Erich Fromm with particular reference to their concept of man.

At this point I should like to summarize briefly a few of the central notions of existentialism, in full awareness of the probability that no two philosophers would agree on the priority of the concepts or their definition. The first idea is that of emptiness or nothingness. A primary question arising in thoughtful man is simply: "Why do I exist, or for that matter, why does anything exist?" Kierkegaard's concern over this problem found expression in his use of the term *Angst,* usually translated as " dread." His attack on the phony religiosity of church-men was echoed in much the same vein by Nietzsche to whom our cathedrals were catacombs for the bones of God, but who still could tremble before the import of his ringing declaration: " God is dead! " Heidegger, in turn, speaks of a " sorrowful concern " with regard to human existence.

The problem of existence was first expressed in modern European consciousness by Descartes's " *Cogito ergo sum* ": a new starting point, but for Europe a disastrous moment ulti-mately eventuating in world war. William Temple convincingly argues that in *Cogito*, Descartes overlooked one third of re-ality. Not only the thinking process and the " I " doing the thinking, but also what the thinking is about — the objective real world — should have been included in the Cartesian so-lution.

Descartes's contemporary, Pascal, though less recognized by succeeding generations for his development of logical and scientific thought, is a more direct ancestor of modern exis-tentialism. Not only is his method of inductive logic more ex-perimentally valid, but his perception and literary expression of man's nothingness is the first cry of *Angst*. Pascal throws man first into contemplation of the infinity of the universe, then sets him to considering the infinite world of the micro-cosm, and concludes: " Whoever shall thus consider himself will be frightened at himself, and observing himself suspended in the mass of matter allotted to him by nature, between these two abysses of infinity and nothingness, will tremble at the sight of these wonders." [1]

A second postulate of existentialism as a philosophy is that the very apparent meaninglessness of existence drives man to search for understanding, meaning, or *rationality*. A third emphasis is that *existence* always precedes essence. This means that man first exists, " turns up on the scene," as Sartre says, before he defines himself with concepts. This is in line with pre-eminently good psychology, for we achieve selfhood; we are not born selves. Further, man is a subject with a self to acquire; he is not merely an object to be known. Man exists; he chooses values and goals. In him as man the *sum* comes before Descartes's *cogito*.

The fourth and fifth ideas of existentialism especially as emphasized by Sartre are *atheism* and *freedom*. Since many atheous thinkers resent being called atheists, as followers of non-Christian religion rightly resent being called pagan, other terms such as " agnostic," " atheous," or " nontheistic " may be preferable. In this postulate, the religious connotation of transcendence as related to God is changed to the need of transcending ourselves toward men horizontally, so to speak, and not in the vertical, theological sense. The frequency of this secular usage of the term " transcendence " should not confuse the theologically oriented reader. Avoiding familiar religious patterns of transcendence, some existential writers urge that man must face and assume his full duties and responsibilities toward self and toward mankind without cluttering his mind with ideas of God.

Man's freedom, of course, in addition to the basic concept of existence, is probably the best-advertised point of existentialism. This may be due to man's subjective yearning for naturalistic, uncomplicated (and often irresponsible) freedom, such as is enacted in the life of the artist Gauguin, or delicately portrayed in the " escape " fantasy of Hudson. It can also be a whistling-in-the-dark type of faith over against the dark, frightening, totalitarian forces at large in the world of modern man. One recent survey of the field, although largely denigrating Kierkegaard, nevertheless shows his influence with its provocative title: *Dreadful Freedom*.[2] In existentialism man's freedom entails his becoming involved in the task of bringing freedom to others. It therefore becomes a basis for responsibility, but when man shrinks from freedom and its ensuing responsibilities he is filled with dread. The thesis of *The Brothers Karamazov*, " Everyone is responsible for everything before everybody," is implicit in much of the existential thinking of the present era.

Existential philosophy, at least in its emphases that are of particular interest to the psychotherapist, has demonstrated that the existence of man is, in its essence, uniquely concrete and subjective. " The factors of uniqueness and singularity are essential constituents of the meaningfulness of human existence. . . . For the presentation of human life as singular and unique is an implicit summons to men to actualize in their own lives these unique and singular possibilities."[3] Max Scheler has described such opportunity for responsible action as dealing with " situational values " that must be realized in the one single opportunity of the particular situation. If one does not use the one unique moment for constructive action, then that particular situational value is never attained or realized. It is of course followed by other situations, but these can never be the same as that one which was passed up. Frankl states the matter in these words: " The meaning of human existence is based upon its irreversible character."[4] The philosophy is eminently religious at this juncture in reminding man that he travels the way of life but once, and in one direction.

Perhaps a simple anecdote at one extreme and the poetic insight of James Russell Lowell at the other can further elaborate the above teaching. Late one evening in a strange city, while looking for a café, I was accosted by a man who asked the price of a meal from me. Reacting as many do to a California " wino," I refused his request and hurried on. Immediately the thought reproached me: " You are hungry, en route to a café. Maybe he, too, is hungry and not panhandling for liquor money." Hurriedly, I retraced my steps, but the man was gone. Thinking he might have turned the corner, I went around the entire block, but never saw him again, though I startled another stranger, asking him if he were the man who had just requested help. This happened twenty years ago, but I clearly recall the uncomfortable feelings that attended my evening snack. Here a particular situational value was never realized.

In therapy, many counselors have been told by patients and clients that they have been saved from desperate action by a simple kindness. Sometimes even a friendly smile from another person has lightened what before had seemed an impossible load. In his account of concentration camp life Frankl says: " I remember how one day a foreman secretly gave me a piece of bread saved from his own breakfast rations. It was far more than a small piece of bread which moved me to tears at the time. It was the human something which this man also gave to me — the word and look that accompanied the gift." Such simple daily " situational values " are open to all men everywhere, under every condition. Of course, more important crises of decision also occur in every life. These have been solemnly described in the familiar poetry of James Russell Lowell: " Once to every man and nation comes the moment to decide."

This cursory and designedly uncritical treatment of a few aspects in the philosophical background of existential analysis is intended chiefly as a point of reference for the therapy itself. Perhaps it may serve a further useful purpose of stimulating the reader to seek further acquaintance with a type of philosophy that speaks with a voice modern man understands. Even the man in the street, untroubled by psychological disputations about the self and altogether cynical about totalitarian causes, can find himself responding with interest to Scheler's affirmation: " Only he who loses himself — in a worthy cause — can gain a genuine self." [5] Perhaps the growing interest in existentialism may be explained in part by man's weariness with the shams and artificialities of his life, and by his desire for a more genuine existence. Existential analysis attempts to actualize a similiar thought of Karl Jaspers': " What a person is, he achieves through the cause which he makes his own." [6] Another central emphasis in Jaspers' teaching echoed by Sartre and others is the challenging proposition that man does not merely exist, but that he is *always deciding* what he will be in the next moment. Thus to the concept of singularness or uniqueness is added the postulate of freedom in terms of decision from moment to moment. In logotherapy, however, Frankl prefers to emphasize responsibility over freedom, for while man is free from something, he is responsible *to* someone, to society, to moral conscience, or to God. Existentialism as a philosophy thus stresses freedom, and is to an extent quite subjective in emphasizing inner values. Logotherapy in stressing responsibility relates the inner values to outer realities.

Existential analysis is phenomenological and voluntaristic in the general psychological sense of these words. Voluntarism makes volition an important character of the mental process. Phenomenology advocates the study of facts or direct experience of facts, or the phenomenon of a human life in its wholeness, at face value, without excluding any factors that may not fit in with a preconceived frame of reference. For example, a chair, to an introspectionist, is an arrangement of lights, colors, and tactual qualities; to physical science it is a mass occupying space; but to a phenomenologist it is just what one perceives it to be, a chair, someplace to sit!

The phenomenological approach to man as *Dasein*, as "human existence," enables existentialist workers stubbornly to reintroduce factors such as man's transcendence over nature and man's feeling that the self is in some sense "spiritual." These and other similar factors long ago were ushered to the edge of oblivion and politely bowed out of existence by a psychology determined to ally itself solely to strict scientific empiricism. Despite sarcastic references to "rat psychology" by exasperated members of the psychological front, it must be admitted that the experimental researchers have compiled an impressive amount of helpful data. But the data on man will never be complete until he is seen in his wholeness as man with a dimension or two that does not submit supinely to measurement, manipulation, and control, as do other animals or objects. Roger Shinn observes succinctly: "Objectivity says that rats in the mazes tell us something about ourselves; *existence* says that they tell us falsehoods if they make us miss the glory and despair of personal life in personal relations." [7]

According to Van der Veldt existential analysts "simply stick to facts. . . ." He suggests that this system remains solely on the empirical level, and avoids the metaphysical implications of existentialist philosophy.[8] Now the first part of this evaluation is descriptive of the phenomenological approach, but the second half must not be misunderstood. If Van der Veldt, who writes from a Catholic viewpoint, is reacting against the atheous group of existentialist philosophers, his conclusion is correct so far as the logotherapy school of existial analysis is concerned. The logotherapy of Frankl faces honestly the question of values, finds religiosity in the unconscious, and leaves the door open for the *Überwelt*, or "transcendence" — an area that is not the primary concern of the medical therapist.

Writing in the *American Journal of Psychotherapy*, W. Van Dusen states a little more accurately the relationship of the existential therapy to the philosophy: "All therapies have a philosophy, but few are so explicit in their relation to a philosophic view of the world as is existential analysis."[9] Even systems that profess to have no values or interest in values still have the "value of no values" or a value that may be called the relativity of all values. If existential analysis would serve no other purpose than that it has called therapy back to a serious consideration of its philosophical background, this alone is sufficient ground for its own existence. If Van Dusen is correct, a therapy without some kind of philosophy simply does not exist. But it is possible for the philosophical orientation of a therapist (particularly as it involves his concept of man) to be so cleverly buried in theory that it is unconsciously used by the therapist in subtle manipulation of his patient! It follows also that it is quite possible for an explicit philosophy to be so poorly chosen that it operates in a derogatory way in therapy.

The relation of philosophy to theory and practice can be compared to the function of a skeletal system in an organism. The bones need to be clothed with the flesh of theory and practice; they must not stick out. If they are absent, you have an amiable jellyfish approach to serious human problems. If they are present, but ignored or unconsciously used, you have the manipulation of the patient that is dangerous for constructive results. This type of thing has been lampooned in the familiar caricature of Carl Rogers' therapy: the client, exasperated by the counselor's apparently meaningless " mirror " responses to all his statements, blurts out: " Who in hell is telling this story, you or me? " The therapist who with the right motivation of removing from a patient his childish, immature religious views can in some cases accomplish this in the wrong way. By a type of spiritual lobotomy he may seek to remove all values along with the basis for values. Existential analysis, particularly as it functions in Frankl's logotherapy with respect to values, is a complement to psychoanalysis, a supplemental aid to psychotherapy.

In logotherapy, the practitioner does not impose his value system upon the patient; while remaining alert to the realm of values, he guides the client along the way of responsibility so that he becomes capable of seeing and choosing his own values. The method has been called " education toward responsibility." [10] In this particular phase of its approach it is similar to Rogers' teaching that the client must be guided toward the capacity of making his own choices, but these must be real, self-conscious decisions, personal to the client. Frankl feels that the aim of the psychotherapist should not be mere health and " adjustment," but it should be to bring out the ultimate possibilities of the patient or client, to help him realize his latent values. The concern of existential philosophy with human existence as singular and unique thus is very pertinent to therapy. The aim of logotherapy is to go beyond the Oedipal strivings of the patient, beyond the inferiority complex and indeed all affect-dynamics. It seeks to get beyond these psychic disturbances of the neurotic in order to get at his spiritual malaise, which is at the core of so many problems of modern man.

Freud once said: " Man has always known that he has a soul. It is my duty to teach him that he also has instincts." How well

Freud succeeded in his teaching is obvious; no one stated the matter more succinctly than Allport, who observed that in the last fifty years sexuality and religiosity have exchanged places. Formerly people freely discussed religious experience but were shy about sex. Today a sophisticated atmosphere prevails concerning sex, but the mention of religion is an occasion for embarrassed silence. This very exchange of places ought to serve as a significant clue for psychotherapy. It indicates that Freud's victory over Victorian mores is complete, for the difficulties that once issued from unresolved, unrecognized sex conflicts now may well be the result of a frustrated and unconscious religiosity! Frankl's *Der Unbewusste Gott* deals with the fact of unconscious religiosity in many people. In it he has an interesting case history of a patient who in a clinical demonstration before a class spoke freely of her intimate sex life. When Frankl mentioned religious experience, she suddenly developed inhibitions and was embarrassed. Seemingly in religious experience shame is a protective force and defensive mechanism preventing the intimate life of the soul from being wholly objectified and manipulated. This is not always a negative value judgment, for, as Frankl observes, love also is an intimate experience. As the roots of the tree must remain in the darkness of the earth so that the tree may live in light, so does the intimate, private life of the individual affect his social and conscious life.

The relevance of values to psychotherapy has aroused the concern not only of philosophers but also of theologians and clergymen, psychiatrists, counselors, and other scientists. Dr. H. Johnson, writing in the *American Journal of Psychiatry*, states: "The central problems of modern Western man are not psychosexual but religio-philosophical. In general they are problems which deal with values. They are problems which raise the question whether life itself is meaningful or without meaning. The problems of contemporary man are no longer the sex and hunger which relate him to the animal but are the varied existential anxieties which arise from the core of man as man." [11] The reticence of many medical men, of the psychotherapist and clinically-oriented counselor, to enter into these problems is understandable. But as Viktor Frankl has pointed out: " He does not ' enter ' these problems; they *come to him* in the despairing attitudes and questions of his patients." Logotherapy urges an honest facing of this situation, and the development of an adequate methodology with which to meet it.

2. Divergent Theory and Some Problems

The present situation in psychotherapy is not unlike that of the man who mounted his horse and rode off in all directions. The theoretical orientation of therapists is based upon widely divergent hypotheses, theories, and ideologies. This sometimes baffles the patient who has to change therapists, and it delights the connoisseur of counseling who shops around to sample the various wares being offered. Individual practitioners of any art are expected to vary, but some well-organized schools of therapy also seem to be working at cross-purposes with other equally well-organized schools. Nevertheless, all schools, given favorable conditions, achieve similar results: the patient or client gets relief and is often enough cured of his disabling difficulties.

Divergence of theory is pointed up in the contrast between the depth psychology of Freud and his followers, with its emphasis upon unconscious influences, and the interference theory of Phillips. This largely ignores unconscious and irrational forces, and it begins therapy with conscious and rational factors in the patient's present experience.[12] It is not without parallel in medical practice where one school treats nephritis, for example, with an extremely low protein diet, and another school seeks to build up the patient and his disabled kidneys with a high protein diet. Patients of both schools get well. No one denies that depth analysis has helped probably many patients to live a more productive and satisfactory life. Interference theory also has an impressive list of case histories to demonstrate its effectiveness as a therapy.

Between the two types of treatment just mentioned, and which I more or less arbitrarily chose as extremes since different ones could serve equally well, the others "waver to and fro" on the battlefield of percept and concept. In addition to therapists who stay relatively close to Freudian orthodoxy, and others who are working in deliberate reaction to Freud's approach, there is a host of eclectic therapists among both psychiatrists and counselors. The latter choose and select from any and all methods of psychotherapy what seems to be most helpful and productive in healing the hurt of man.

Freud's monumental place in psychotherapy is a well-established fact that does not need any embellishments of defense. Even the violence of some of the attacks on his system proves the point, for intelligent men do not waste time demolishing mere men of straw. What Karl Marx has done to and with political theory and economic theory Sigmund Freud has done in the field of mental health. In terms of permanent influence in history and in medical arts, both men are well established. One could spend many pages detailing the brilliance, extraordinary acumen, and depth of insight of the doctor in Freud, but there is no need for that in a book of this type. What remains more interesting to a therapist from the historical and biographical viewpoint is the man himself, his personality and what made him "tick." But no mere student who knew the man as a teacher, nor one who may have mastered the literature and method of psychoanalysis, is capable of telling the full story of Freud. Perhaps only his very close intimate, Ludwig Binswanger, could give us an analytic biography of the man himself, for, as Rollo May has said, "Binswanger was the only colleague who dared to differ with him, and with whom he yet maintained friendship."

The suggestion of a lonely, creative genius comes as no surprise to those familiar with the master's authoritarian milieu. The violent breaks between Freud and the more prominent of his early disciples who established schools of their own bears this out. The true church always has excommunicated the heretics! But it ought also to be said that Freud suffered the fate of many a pioneer into new areas of thought or action. He was violently criticized, and to this criticism he reacted vigorously. It is just possible that had clergymen, for instance, not attacked him with the "science falsely so-called" approach but had listened patiently while reserving the judgments that come so quickly, Freud might have mellowed with regard to religion. On the other hand, when his earliest American disciple, Prof. James J. Putnam, of Harvard, urged a deeper consideration of metaphysical elements in psychoanalysis, his suggestions were, as we have seen, dismissed by Freud.

Today most psychoanalysts themselves are in the forefront of those who maintain that analysis as a treatment method has strict limitations not only as to the time it takes but also as to the clientele. They are well aware that many patients are not good subjects for analysis, and these facts alone should warn ardent admirers among clergy who have recently discovered it not to expect too much from it. They stand to gain more from a study of its profound insights into human nature than from an imitation of its techniques without adequate training. Analysts, therefore, are also interested to see that other schools of therapy develop in order to help carry the load.

A familiar difficulty that analysts and, to some extent, all therapists face today is the superficial knowledge and semantic ramifications that have resulted from popular writings on analytical procedure. The playwrights discovered it first, decades ago, but now all who can read and listen are fairly bathed in a backwash of popularized and often distorted ideas of analysis that reaches even into the paperback detective story aimed at the juvenile. The best of this is reflected in the humor of the numerous psychiatric jokes, which in itself demonstrates the pervasiveness, if not depth, of public interest. This superficial analytic knowledge often enough results in a patient's coming to the therapist after having wandered intellectually through a jungle of psychological verbiage. This has given him no insight into his difficulties, for the rational terminology or knowledge has not been able to get through to his emotional life where his sickness is active. The analyst, therapist, or counselor must first cut his own way through this jungle to get at the personality of his patient. When he deals with a highly educated patient, this involves certain fencing or sparring, with resultant waste of time or postponement of effective treatment.

Other difficulties of analysis are reported by those with resources to try out the different schools. Their depth recollections and dreams were considerably different under Jungian treatment than they were when under Freudian treatment. As a child tries to please teacher, it is inevitable that a patient, sensitively aware of his doctor's theoretical background, on occasions at least will also try to " please " his analyst. Other nonanalytical therapies may be able to detour around this particular problem, but it can be a factor to reckon with in any orientation. There are also other technical and personal difficulties of analysis, concerning which Robert Lindner has written with most honest and courageous self-revelation.[13]

Just about the time that Americans were discovering the existential writings of Kierkegaard, Continental psychiatrists and psychoanalysts began to examine the relevance of existentialism and psychotherapy. Coincidentally, this same period, from about 1925 to 1950, was also the time that Freudian influence reached an all-time peak of popularity and publicity in America. Everyone is acquainted with the concurring tidal wave of self-help books, and the omnipresent psychological articles in popular magazines extolling the omnipotence of psychology. This created in the popular mind the pathetic credulity that a bygone generation once had in the efficacy of patent medicine. The process has continued to such an extent that at a recent conference in San Francisco a psychiatrist complained bitterly: " Psychiatry has been vastly oversold. People come with the expectation of a magic cure-all." Large industrial corporations have reacted to the influence by adding psychi-

atrists to their staffs, and by calling upon psychologists to help
them select and maintain the morale of their personnel. The
multimillion-dollar public relations and advertising industry
has gone into depth analysis in a big way, using the results of
what is called "motivation analysis" to manipulate the unwary consumer. This manipulation is done deliberately and
cynically, or sometimes with an uneasy conscience as to the
long-term results.[14]

The popularity of psychology inevitably resulted in the
victimization of many people by self-advertised experts in
counseling, marriage problems, and vocational adjustment.
The indiscriminate use of psychological tests by such people
occasionally does serious personality damage that genuine
experts labor long to repair. One of my students made a survey
of the advertising "psychological experts" in a major American
city. Out of fifteen whom he investigated, only one had had
any advanced training, a master's degree in psychology. Most
of the remainder had had little or no college education. One,
a former chiropractor, used the Rorschach test as his chief
technical aid, and readily confessed that he had "studied up
on the test" by himself. A thorough discussion of this problem
appeared a few years ago and exposed some of the charlatans
at work in psychology.[15] That such activity can exist on the
fringe of bona fide therapeutic work shows the widespread
need for psychotherapy and for sharing the work not only
among medical men but also among other trained specialists.

Many universities and several theological schools are providing excellent training for men who are entering the various
fields of counseling. But even though this training may eventuate in the doctor of philosophy degree with a major in psychological counseling, it does not equip one to handle cases
that call for medical or psychiatric diagnosis and treatment.
The nonmedical counselor and the pastor should be thoroughly
grounded in psychopathology so that he can recognize not only
obvious but incipient somatic and psychotic disturbances, and
refer the client to a medically trained specialist. It is customary

for the skilled counselor to insist on a medical examination of the client when embarking upon extended counseling in order to detect and have treated any possible somatic causes of personality disturbances. It is obviously useless for a counselor or psychiatrist to deal with the difficulties of a patient when these are the result of a malfunction of the thyroid gland, or due to paresis. Frankl himself has done research in the field of the hyperfunction of thyroid glands resulting in pseudoagoraphobic states. This research has shown the way to the treatment of such cases by drug therapy utilizing, for example, tranquilizers that he developed in Vienna.

The professional training of the medical practitioner, the surgeon, and the psychiatrist equips them with special skills and knowledge to which the counselor defers when he refers a client. These skills include diagnostic ability, medical and drug therapy, surgery, occasionally the use of projective tests, psychoanalysis, etc. Shock therapy and prefrontal or transorbital lobotomy could also be mentioned here, but happily these radical forms of treatment are falling into disuse, at least as indiscriminate "cures" of emotional ills. Many psychiatrists, however well grounded in neurology and psychiatry, have received in their basic training very little psychology. Some medical schools still provide only a single-semester course in medical psychology for their students in the four-year training period. Here the clinical psychologist, trained in projective and diagnostic tests as well as in psychotherapy, can complement the work of the psychiatrist. In the well-organized hospital he is a valuable member, along with the psychiatric social worker, of the psychiatric team.

The interrelationships between medicine, psychiatry, clinical psychology, and counseling are developing to the point where in many communities the various disciplines complement one another's work. This is not merely an idealized frame of reference; it happens to be the *modus vivendi* of many psychotherapists, counselors, and pastors. The writer is a clinical psychologist, and a teacher in a theological school. Teaching and counseling duties permit only a small private practice, but a significant proportion of this includes referrals from medical doctors, psychiatrists, and pastors of local churches. An interesting development in co-operation is the increasing number of seminar discussions held on a regular monthly basis through the country between psychiatrists, ministers, and counselors. Not the least of the results is for psychoanalysts to learn that not all religious phenomena are morbid or immature projections, and for pastors to learn that psychiatrists are not disciples of the " Adversary."

The broad view of psychotherapy as mentioned earlier is certainly descriptive of the actual state of affairs today. To prevent the victimization of an unwary public, in addition to state licensing or other legal controls the moral force of a specialized Hippocratic oath for psychotherapists might be considered by the professional organizations. By way of another essay at definition, it should be emphasized that psychotherapy is not so much an occasion for problem-solving, or even for the cure of mental disease, as it is an *opportunity* for the patient to *grow* so that motivation operates on ever higher levels. Then the patient or client is enabled to work out new patterns of living that enable him to take the problems, perplexities, frustrations, or sufferings that life has to offer, as a mature adult would take them. The problem of meaningful existence, which the philosopher may often enough be able to handle in a detached way, permits no such detachment to the therapist. The doctor diagnosing an incurable carcinoma, the counselor with a suicidal client, the pastor comforting inconsolable grief — these all face the problem of meaning in the most existential of ways.

How the problem of meaning is related to therapy is one of the areas where logotherapy, that is, the existential school of Frankl, will have much to offer. The total pressure of modern life sharpens this issue whether we consider it from the aspect of individual anxiety and neurosis or in the light of national and international tensions resulting from prevailing political climate and technological progress. It is an easy paraphrase of Tennyson's words to assert that more people live by anxiety than this world dreams of. "The spiritual disintegration of our day consists in the loss of an ultimate meaning of life by the people of Western civilization. And with the loss of the meaning of life they have lost personality and community. They have become, whether they know it or not, parts of an objective process that determines their life in every respect, from their economic situation to their spiritual form. The insecurities and vicissitudes involved in this process have produced feelings of fear, anxiety, loneliness, abandonment, uncertainty, and emptiness. Their spiritual life oscillates between a cynical and fanatical surrender to powers the nature of which nobody can fully grasp or control, and the end of which nobody can foresee." [16] Tillich, philosopher of religion and history, saw the cynical turning of Germany's youth to Nazism as one illustration of the loss of meaning. Other indications could be cited, such as our pervading reverence for material success, or the continuous increase in the percentage of youthful inmates in our corrective institutions. Playwrights often enough have dramatized the problem, from T. S. Eliot's *The Cocktail Party*, to Tennessee Williams' *Cat on a Hot Tin Roof*, and novelists find ample material in modern "mass man," "organization man," as they deal satirically with some frustrations of personality that seem to be inherent in business organization. Albert Camus sketches the matter incisively in his novel *The Fall*.

3. Unifying Factors in Psychotherapy

The layman may be confused as to how diametrically opposed ideas of therapy can have equal success in helping people break the confining chains of neurosis. Psychoanalysis, with a deterministic view of man controlled by deep unconscious forces, cures by exorcising the demons from the unconscious with its well-known method. Interference theory, other voluntaristic schools, and some existential ones, tend to ignore unconscious forces, and make a rational attack on present difficulties. The factor they have in common is a significant relationship between the therapist and his client, though there are crucial differences in the mode of relating. However, it is one thing to agree on the necessity of relationship, and quite another to achieve it in practice.

One can read volumes on rapport, and still be defeated as a practitioner by personal dynamics, aloof or urbane attitudes. Professionalism can just as easily be the error of the psychiatrist as it may be the sin of the minister. On the amusing side, Carroll Wise and J. C. Wynn have described the unsophisticated young pastor, sitting on the edge of his chair, breathlessly awaiting the lurid details of a personal confession, and thus unwittingly allowing his curiosity to defeat his attempt at counseling. This sort of thing is not entirely without parallel in psychiatry also, as some doctors are willing to admit.

A dichotomy of objectivity and concern seems to be involved in the therapeutic relationship. Objectivity gives one the advantage of an observation point, but then psychotherapy is a matter of seeking insight into personal involvement. Objectivity points to truth and meaning, but in psychotherapy these can be grasped only in personal concern and in the intensity of personal experience.

Only personality can reach the depth of the existence of any other person. Ideas, for example, always remain abstract until they are incarnated in persons or personal issues. A law really becomes part of the code only after it has been tested in the courts with an issue involving persons and experiences. In therapy, regardless of the theoretical orientation of the doctor, a most important therapeutic element remains — that of the relationship that involves vital, dynamic attitudes to be shared by two people. These two people tend to come to a common viewpoint or experience of some very important (though not necessarily all) aspects of life, *and of each other's being.* The existence of each is significantly affected, deepened, and made more meaningful, by virtue of having shared vital elements of the self in the experience of relationship.

The psychoanalyst Dr. Lindner candidly tells how he became so earnestly involved in treating a psychotic patient that he almost "went over the line" himself in rapport with his patient and the intricately fascinating, delusional mathematical system he had built up. Yet the doctor's dangerous concern was the turning point in the patient's road to recovery. The nondirective counselor too remains responsible for choosing *which* statements of the client to reflect or to draw out for further expression. Carl Rogers has made it very clear that client-centered technique involves the experience of the deep sharing in relationship of two persons. The most couch-centered analyst who stays out of sight nevertheless reveals something of himself to the alert patient by the very inflection of his voice. The most introvert of nondirective counselors, who fears something of his own personality may creep into the interview, if he is to help the client, must establish the relationship that is at the center of the therapeutic process. I refer here to shy and inexperienced counselors who have been known to misuse Rogers' excellent method to avoid the responsiblity of entering fully into the counseling situation. Thus they parody the approach by inane responses, many of which have been the butt of humorous anecdotes.

Relationship is not a static thing, nor a matter of theory and technique. A Kantian might say it is the "categorical imperative" of the whole business, an a priori! In fact, a therapist whose technique is faulty can succeed in curing a patient, but only when his attitudes have been basically correct. Some authoritarian counselors whose personal attitudes achieve sucessful relationships thereby succeed in spite of their dogmatic approach. This lays them open to the charge by orthodox psychoanalysts that they remain benign father figures to their patients! On the other hand, a therapist with excellent technique, based on widely accepted theory, can easily fail if his attitudes operate to make a real relationship with the patient impossible. The attitude of the aloof, or too urbane, doctor can create more anxiety and aggression in his patient.

In the state hospital, residents in psychiatry, if they are concerned about sick people, learn fast. If they are there merely to learn to classify and diagnose, and to pass the board examinations, while despising the disorganized minds they "have to practice on," the results are soon evident, not only in the attitudes of patients, but in the personality structures of the doctors themselves. Even a psychotic person becomes aware and recognizes when he is being treated as an object that can be manipulated or ignored at another's whim. I can never forget the scorching lines of a bitter poem once written by a brilliant but definitely psychotic young man in a large hospital where I was working as a clinician. It is true, the hospital was badly overcrowded, and perhaps it is harder for busy people to be concerned people. But it was easy, and uncomfortable, to recognize ourselves — doctors, attendants, and other professional workers — in the poet's lines as he delineated the attitudes of professionalism, the hearty (and false) assurance, the meaningless slap on the back, the promises broken because they were made to a psychotic! As Viktor Frankl has insisted, a man may be mentally ill and still be right, and he adds, "Two and two still make four even when a psychotic says so!"

A common experience for psychiatrists, counselors, and pastoral confessors, for that matter, is the feeling of utter exhaustion after a series of interviews. Maybe they echo in feeling the statement of the devout young priest who came from his first confessions lamenting: "O God, I am sickened by the sins of these people!" Or maybe exhaustion is a necessary correlate to good counseling or confession because something *has gone out* of the therapist or priest into the patient, something of value, of significance or meaning. And due to the uniqueness of personality, every skilled therapist readily admits that he gains or learns from each and every interview, whether it is with a learned colleague or with a disorganized mind, or even with a mentally retarded person.

What helps to actualize relationship between doctor and

patient is not a theory or technique, but the genuine acceptance of the patient, and the permissive atmosphere that is thereby created. And though acceptance and permissiveness are very vital doctrines, particularly of counseling therapy, the doctor does not begin with them as theory, but rather, he *enacts* them in his attitudes toward his patient. When, as a result, rapport is successfully established, then, and often enough only then, *for the first time in his entire life* the patient is *free to be himself.* He can really be himself with all his fears, anxieties, guilt, weakness, self-loathing, and distrust, all because of a relationship established with another person who accepts him as he really is without moralizing, without criticizing or judging him. The therapist in turn accepts him with the sole purpose of helping him to grow out of his weaknesses and perplexities into a more mature life or meaningful existence.

Now a therapist cannot help a patient develop any further, in last analysis, than he himself has proceeded in his own personality development and *Weltanschauung.* Here the necessity for psychotherapists to deal with philosophical presuppositions and even religion seems inescapable. In *permissiveness* is indicated the attitude and/or activity by which the therapist creates the atmosphere wherein the patient can progressively and constructively be honest with himself. Can a therapist be any the less honest with his own self? Psychiatrists, while remaining agnostic themselves, occasionally recommend faith or religion to their patients. Here certainly is a serious inconsistency, to recommend one " illusion " as a cure for other illusions! A doctor should be able to conceive of the possibility of his contracting the same disease as his patient and accordingly should be willing to take the same prescription. Or to put it simply, if the patient has religious needs, does not the doctor also? Or are there two radically different classes of beings, doctors and patients? Frankl in his logotherapy faces this dilemma boldly and is not afraid to pronounce the name of God clearly and in personalistic terms.

The religious-education emphasis in all branches of Protestant and Catholic and Jewish faith holds that the child only learns of God and the love of God as that love is mediated through the attitudes of his parents or parent figures. Even as a parent mediates the love of God to the child, the psychiatrist mediates the patience of God to the sick person. Whether or not the psychiatrist is aware of this, the fact remains that he is playing a significant role in the medical care of souls. Tillich has spelled this out in plain language: " In depth psychology there is frequently more awareness of the meaning of grace and, consequently, more effective 'care of souls' than in the ministry of the church." [17] Since Tillich is an experienced minister, as well as a long-time student of psychotherapy and a philosopher, he has ample authority for making his statement.

Erich Fromm, even though speaking from a naturalistic standpoint, boldly lifts the Scriptural injunction to 'love your neighbor as yourself' from its context to assert that is the most important norm for living. In order that I may not be accused of taking Fromm out of context, let him speak more fully: " There is no more convincing proof that the injunction ' Love thy neighbor as thyself ' is the most important norm for living, and that its violation is the basic cause of unhappiness and mental illness, than the evidence gathered by the psychoanalyst. Whatever complaints the neurotic patient may have, whatever symptoms he may present, are rooted in his inability to love if we mean by love a capacity for the experience of concern, responsibility, respect, and understanding of another person and the intense desire for that person's growth. Analytic therapy is essentially an attempt to help the patient to gain or regain his capacity for love. If this aim is not fulfilled, nothing but surface changes can be accomplished." [18]

If I were a psychoanalyst with the usual clientele of educated or cultivated patients, I would embellish and frame the last two sentences of Fromm's words cited above, and hang them in a conspicuous place in my office for all patients to see. Since many patients come with relatively superficial ideas of what analysis involves, and are forearmed, as was mentioned earlier, with a glib psychological vocabulary of escape, Fromm's cogent statement would place responsibility squarely where it belongs. He goes on in his Yale lectures to broaden the concept of love by insisting that love by its very nature cannot be restricted to one person. Walter Lippmann scores the same point when he says that people who marry for love and nothing else very soon have the nothing else. This is obviously because their love is the immature type that focuses upon one person for what that person can give them.

Fromm's use of the familiar text, "Love your neighbor as yourself," closely parallels the usual exegesis of these words given by the minister of religion. Enlightened Judaism and Christianity always have taught a doctrine of love that breaks down into the spectrum of "concern, responsibility, respect, and understanding of another person," though admittedly, teaching and practice often are some distance apart. Fromm's reminder that "love for one person [only] is an attachment of submission or of domination but not love," is a negative rendering of much of the Old Testament prophet's emphasis upon social justice.

Whenever psychiatric writings discuss love as a dynamic in establishing effective personal relationships, whether these be the acceptance between therapist and patient or the attitudes of the patient toward other people, it would seem that psychotherapy comes quite close to the borders of religious teaching. Of course the church has no monopoly on love, and it would be absurd even to make such an inference. Perhaps love has been expounded too facilely by the clergy as a doctrine (something to "believe" in) while therapists have quietly impounded love as a dynamic force in their professional practice. How otherwise explain the fact that many people freely take problems to a doctor that they "would never dream of bringing to the pastor"? Is this due to secularism of the people or to their stereotype of the pastor as official conscience of the community? The therapist has *earned* a confidence by *enacting* his acceptance, whereas many people fear and expect judgmental attitudes from their pastor. Mature religious experience always has known love is more than a doctrine, and in every generation it has exemplified the power of love. Skill in counseling people with their emotional problems as well as with their spiritual difficulties has also been demonstrated by many pastors.

The above statements are not designed to call attention to either the failures or the superiorities of psychotherapy and religion, one against another. The intent is to map out the frontier area of human existence where both practice the art of helping people in trouble. Since they meet each other on the doorstep of the sick soul, *rapprochement*, or at least the allaying of mutual suspicion, is highly desirable. Attention was deliberately called to the therapist's enactment of attitudes of permissiveness, acceptance, and so on, because of their central significance in achieving relationship, with its consequent therapeutic good for the patient. In religion, at least in its Judaeo-Christian tradition, the original understanding of salvation was that God unconditionally *accepts* the sinner, and this in spite of his sin. But this is only the negative half of the truth. The positive half is that God accepts, not merely " to save the sinner from hell," but because he knows the ultimate potential and meaning of which the sinner's life is capable. In the matter of establishing relationship, the pastoral counselor of course carries the matter into the transcendent realm, for he believes that God also is involved in the relationship and that God seeks to establish or accomplish his purpose in and through human relationship. How and when the transcendent is to enter the therapeutic relationship becomes a vital matter to the pastoral counselor. He does not depend solely upon prayer to unravel a tangled marital situation any more than a psychiatrist would recommend lobotomy to relieve deep distress caused by vocational conflicts or Oedipal fixations. The New Testament word translated " to save " also means " to heal " or " to make whole," whereas the whole Biblical emphasis on salvation includes spiritual maturation as much as anything else.

4. The Ultimate Goal of Psychotherapy

A difficult area in which to look for some semblance of agreement or unity of purpose is the ultimate goal of the therapeutic process. When the matter of goals or ultimates comes up it has been too easy in the past to retreat behind the defenses of scientific objectivity and to leave that sort of thing to philosophy or religion. The modern world moves too fast for even the therapist to ignore these things, particularly in view of their influence upon patient and client. The rocket that was Dr. Goddard's scientific toy in one decade became Hitler's threat to England in another decade, and scant years later put an artificial satellite into orbit around the earth. An interesting mathematical formula, eventuated in a few short years in nuclear fission and fusion that in turn can either devastate our world or provide unlimited power and productivity for all nations of the world. The end of the matter will not be the result of blind chance or a necessary response to an unavoidable stimulus, but rather the result of the decisions of responsible men. The question remains before us as to whether man is the helpless victim of environmental forces without and driven by unconscious forces within, or whether he is capable of reacting spontaneously to the world in terms of freedom, responsibility, and personal decision. Existential philosophy and logotherapy give the answer in terms of freedom, responsibility, and decision.

The simple answer to the question of goal is this: therapy aims at mental health and happiness through the relief of anxiety, the allaying of guilt feelings, the handling of repressed hostility, and so on. Fromm has related unhappiness and mental sickness to the failure to gain a capacity for love. Is not, then, the removal of unhappiness and the cure of mental sickness goal enough for psychotherapy? The answer to this question must be in the negative. Even assuming that some forms of mental illness can be cured in a given patient, there often are deep neurotic conditions resulting from somatic illnesses that resist treatment. Upon the therapist then falls the responsibility of helping the patient to live over and beyond the effects of the illness. One sees this achievement in some sufferers from inoperable carcinoma who nevertheless arrive at such serenity that they defeat their illness long before that illness defeats their body.

If psychotherapy takes the guarantee of happiness as a goal, it steps out of its role just as surely as it must when it overlaps onto philosophical or religious territory. For one thing, the founding fathers of our country were more cautious in discussing the rights of man. They included as a right, only the *pursuit* of happiness, for happiness is not an entity. One does not pursue it as if he were searching for a collar button that has rolled under the table! Happiness is never an end in itself but rather, a side effect of devotion to more important and unselfish goals. In marriage counseling, a familiar lament is the charge that one partner had failed to make the other happy. Of course trouble is bound to ensue if two people marry with the romantic expectation that marriage is an automatic guarantee of happiness. Marriage is a fairly old institution of the human race, and it was not designed with happiness as a primary consideration. Psychotherapy is a fairly old institution too (if we are prepared to admit the witch doctor as our forebear) and it also should not take happiness for a primary goal.

The therapist himself has few experiences that can transcend the deep satisfaction and happiness of seeing an analysis or extended counseling eventuate in a new, reorganized, constructive personality. To be instrumental in changing an unhappy, disorganized, anxiety-ridden individual into an organized self capable of better utilization of emotional and intellectual potentialities is to share in the work of creation itself. The goal of a total self, the full personality potential, becomes the centrum or lever that must be brought to bear on the treatment of inner conflicts. In therapy everything is relevant and nothing is insignificant, for here we are dealing with personality in its many-faceted form. A diamond must be cut with a minimum number of sixty-four facets to reflect light properly and thus show its purity and beauty, but the therapist in dealing with human personality works with far more than sixty-four facets!

Erich Fromm in his stimulating and concerned writing describes self-realization in terms of positive freedom as the spontaneous activity of the total integrated personality. "Most of us can observe at least moments of our own spontaneity which are at the same time moments of genuine happiness. Whether it be the fresh and spontaneous perception of a landscape, or the dawning of some new truth as the result of our thinking, or a sensuous pleasure that is not stereotyped, or the welling up of love for another person, in these moments we all know what a spontaneous act is and may have some vision of what a human life could be if these experiences were not such rare and uncultivated occurrences." [19] In each of the moments that Fromm describes, the subjective experience of happiness is a by-product of the spontaneous perception of the larger, objective reality. To cultivate the patient's capacity for such perceptions is also the work of the therapist.

In undertaking therapy it follows that the psychotherapist is assuming responsibility for helping another person come to a fuller understanding, integration, and expression of the potentials of which his own unique life is capable. When I undergo surgery, I do not expect my surgeon to guarantee either my life or the "success" of the operation, for much if not all of surgery is diagnostic. But I do expect my doctor to assume responsibility for seeing that the best of all that is known in procedure will be done in my behalf. Furthermore, I know that he is personally concerned over my welfare, not merely as a patient, but as a human being. Psychotherapy must evidence similar responsibility and concern all the more because its procedure is less dramatic and more subtle than that of surgery. Carl Rogers has insisted carefully that responsibility for choice of action, goals, use of therapy time, must rest upon the patient, lest he grow in dependence on the counselor rather than in the experience of responsibility for his own activity. Yet the responsibility of the psychotherapist remains the more vital because of the far-reaching influence of what happens, or may fail to happen, during therapy. If our discussion of respect for the person of the client and of the relationship in therapy has real significance, then the therapist risks himself, his very being, in therapy. Every success and every failure in therapy inevitably affects the doctor as well as the patient! His duty is to draw the real essence of his patient into the therapeutic relationship, but he cannot do this effectively without letting his own real personality become involved also.

It follows that scientific detachment, or " objectivity," can at times be the antithesis of therapy. A paradox is evident here in the danger of losing the value of objectivity, resulting in the therapist's developing a " Jehovah complex," or the other extreme of allowing empathy to become maudlin sympathy and rapport to degenerate into a mere mush of amiability. The answer may lie in viewing objectivity qualitatively rather than quantitatively. A therapist may often spend his fifty minutes uttering scarcely a word. Yet all the while he has been giving himself in his attitudes, and exposing these attitudes in mannerisms, expression, and tone of voice to the sensitive patient. The exquisite poetry of Martin Buber's prose in *I and Thou* provides a helpful concept here: The I of the patient is called into being by the Thou of a skillful therapist. But is not the therapist, as I also affected by the Thou of the patient?

The goal of psychotherapy would seem to be inclusive at least of mental health, happiness, and self-realization, and in working toward these the responsibility of the therapist requires the involvement of his total self. In conventional Freudian analysis, the aim is to bring into awareness the contents of the personal unconscious that are related to or are the cause of present difficulties. Freud first saw the unconscious as the repository of repressed, painful, and unpleasant experiences and drives, and held that therapy proceeds by bringing these into consciousness. In Jung, the scope of the unconscious is much greater, containing much more than merely repressed material, and also holding items that can never be brought into consciousness. To Jung, the unconscious, no mere dumping ground of the conscious mind, is vital to the very functioning of the conscious, an important source of its energy, as it were. It also contains positive material such as memories, childhood experiences, religious experiences, early ideals, dreams, vivid impressions. Erich Fromm also teaches that the unconscious is a repository of positive, good elements as well as negative things. The ego is necessarily limited by the contents of the conscious mind, but the totality of man's psychic nature, labeled "*Seele*," or "soul," by Jung, is not exhausted by what in American psychology is known as "personality," for it includes all the resources and energies of the unconscious. For orthodox psychoanalysis, then, there is no possibility of attaining mental health, happiness, or self-realization until the unconscious is thoroughly explored, its powerful drives and influences carefully analyzed, sublimated, and reoriented.

The neo-orthodox school of analysis, represented by Fromm, Karen Horney, and many other practitioners, has given excellent insight into the masochistic, defensive, and aggressive elements of neurotic suffering. Instead of realizing the potentials of the self, the neurotic loses himself in his suffering, in his fantasies, in his mental pain. This results in a definite type of satisfaction that is his way of adjusting to the society in which he lives, and to the drives within himself for status and domination. The neurotic, like all immature persons, wants the fruits of personality without being willing or able to pay the price of responsibility. "Suffering and helplessness become his outstanding means of obtaining affection, help, control, and at the same time allow him to evade all demands that others might make on him. Suffering has finally the function of expressing accusations against others in a disguised but effective way. Neurotic suffering, inasmuch as it serves certain functions, is not what the person wants, but what he pays, and the satisfaction he aims at is not suffering itself, but a relinquishment of the self." [20]

Other psychoanalysts such as Alexander and Guntrip, with

many years of experience in therapy with neurotics, come to
similar conclusions as to the significance of the neurotic handling of the problem of attaining self-realization. The neurotic
presents us with a reverse image of personality development.
As the abnormal always gives us a photographic enlargement
of normal processes, the suffering of the neurotic serves to
point up what can be called the *dialectic demand* on personality, a demand that the neurotic can see only as a dilemma.
The whole thrust of Western civilization in its historical development, its culture, psychology, politics, economics, and religion, tinctured as it is with Eastern mysticism, makes us heirs
of this dialectic demand upon personality. Briefly stated, it is
simply that the self can realize itself only by losing itself. In
living experience this is not really a difficult paradox. That a
man can rise above selfish concerns and obtain satisfaction by
losing himself in something greater than himself has been an
age-old experience of mature members of the race. Professor
Frankl insists that " existence is characterized above all by the
ability of man to transcend himself. Thus man is able to objectify and even to oppose himself." As he pointed out in the
recent World Congress of Psychotherapy held at Barcelona,
" man is only close to himself to the extent that he is close to
the things of the world, to the extent that he stands in and for
the world." [21]

The dialectic demand still appears to be a dilemma to many,
however. This is because our democratic idealism in politics,
sociology, philosophy, psychology, and religion all stress the
deep need for individuation. The process of becoming an individual is started by the infant's assertion of himself against
the authority of the parents. The intrinsic and incalculable
worth of the person as an individual self is an ideology rooted
far more deeply in the past than the wresting of the Magna
Carta from King John of England. The American Bill of Rights,
our system of justice, the log-cabin tradition of the Presidency,
all are a direct outcome of the idea of the infinite value of the
individual person. The present cold war chills us the more by

virtue of the fact that there is now prevalent in the world another ideology that completely disregards the value of the person as individual existence. This ideology emphasizes the tremendous value of the state and the complete insignificance of individuals.

Complicating the Western ideology is the fact that in our competitive society the individual is expected to fight his own battles, stand on his own feet, and on the head of his fellow man if that is necessary to climb the ladder of "success." Healthy competition in athletics is matched by unhealthy competition for grades in those academic systems where education is measured by the compilation of facts and the "passing" of required courses rather than by the stimulus of ideas. Religion is no exception in the competitive race. The success of the clergyman is measured by the number of conversions, the size of the crowds, of the church, of the budget. Because of the competition here, every clergyman knows how truly a certain saint spoke: "The besetting sin of the clergy is jealousy."

It is no wonder, then, in neurosis the individual finds the dialectic demand confusing and too difficult to meet with its many-sided challenge. Instead of losing the self, *he dissolves the self;* he allows the self to go into solution: the crystals of his personality potential are dissolved in his own inner solution of fantasy and suffering. The oblivion of the self is his answer to the confusing call of our culture to rise to the responsibilities of true maturity. More or less benign forms of this are seen in the student who, faced with ever-mounting requirements of essays and examinations, comes to his counselor puzzled by an overwhelming need for excessive amounts of sleep. The shy wife, whose husband's promotion now requires more social activity than she feels herself capable of, suffers the agony of migraine headaches. Skid Row of San Francisco and other cities occasionally includes among its derelicts brilliant men whose neurotic conflicts have driven them into this form of escape, into oblivion of the self with its inexorable and haunting demands for development and fulfillment. Alcoholism, amnesia, and masochism often are forms of neurotic suffering related primarily to the self, and only secondarily to other persons or objects.

Biography abundantly illustrates the way in which the individual achieves self-realization by losing the self in a great cause. Harry Overstreet feels strongly, therefore, that biography has been neglected in the schools as a method of teaching history and values. Science certainly has stimulated the modern imagination; it also provides us with an impressive array of devoted men and women whose unselfish giving of their whole being (and sometimes their lives) to research, is richly illustrative. In the past, religion offered ways of losing self for a cause, but today, according to Karen Horney, " it has lost its appeal for the majority." [22] Maybe she is right — for the majority; but individual exceptions are numerous. The heroic story of Albert Schweitzer is matched by the recent widely publicized martyrdom of missionaries to the primitive Auca Indians of South America.[23] An architect of my acquaintance gave up a promising career, learned theology and aviation, in order to become a member of the foreign service of his church. After twenty years of work, educational, medical, and religious, amidst the squalor and primitive conditions of Brazilian backlands, he reported how a deep satisfaction in his work continued to grow through the years.[24] Such people, of course, are not in the majority, but they are " majoring " in life — they call it eternal life — and in history their significance has always made up for their lack in numbers. Frankl speaks of but two races of man, the decent and the indecent, and holds that where formerly faith in automatic progress made optimism easy, today our pessimism, or awareness that decent people remain a minority, challenges us to join this minority. Thus he would utilize the pessimism of our day to evoke activism in contrast to old-fashioned optimism that resulted in complacency.

When the self remains the center of reference — with its conflicts, limitations, anxieties, doubts, and pains — even the neurotic cannot stand such a self, and he seeks to get rid of it in the amazing variety of types of neurotic suffering described in analytic literature. The dialectic demand of realizing the self through losing it in the service of a greater reality, through mastery and creativity, through allegiance to other persons, issues, and causes, remains the requirement of our culture. Through psychoanalytic concepts of unconscious life and in the intimacy of analysis have come profound insights on the depths of human nature. These have passed over into other disciplines besides psychotherapy and counseling. But even for medical therapy, a rational and emotional grasping of the significance of the past and its power over the present is not enough. A new orientation to the past, the present, and above all to the future is vital. To put it succinctly, the patient needs not only to be cured of present illness, he also needs goals for the future. He must find the utmost meaning for his life. Client-centered counseling insists that a responsibility of the therapist is to assist the client to grow and mature to the point where he is progressively able to choose meaningful goals for himself.

It would appear, then, that self-realization, unless carefully qualified in the mind and aim of the therapist, can no more be the goal of therapy than either health or happiness. All of us know people who are exuberantly healthy but who remain clods that never develop a fraction of their potentialities. Familiar too is the "happy" person who lives a vegetative existence with no concern for the values that make men human beings. The realized self too is no monad, an isolated pillar of perfection. That is as much a parody of human development as that of the man who is proud of his humility. Like the beautiful Corinthian pillars of a Greek temple, self-realization has meaning only in its relation to a larger purpose of function.

This chapter closes with a final question: Can psychotherapy progress very much farther, can it truly fulfill its function and be a real healing force, without developing a more adequate concept of man? Or since, in Allport's phrase, man always is in a process of becoming, should not psychotherapy be continuously at work, developing a deeper approach to the nature of the man it proposes to heal? Can science accomplish this task alone with its instruments of logic, measurement, prediction, research, and observation? Or can science co-operate with the imaginative, intuitive approach of philosophy and religion, and draw upon their insights into the nature of man?

The method of science necessarily involves treating all that it handles as objects to manipulate and measure. The idea of treating man as an object causes increasing concern in medical and psychological circles. Carl Rogers has written penetratingly upon this problem.[25] Theologians agree that, due to his transcendence, God cannot properly be defined, for definitions are based upon comparison, and there is no *thing* with which we can compare God.[26] We have a similar problem in trying to measure man, who is himself the "measure of all things." True, man belongs to the animal kingdom, but what makes him distinctly human is precisely the most distinctly nonanimal part of his being. It is obvious that the extensive research of the animal psychologists adequately establishes this fact. The founder of logotherapy refers to animals as "representatives of mere psychophysical being," but he sees man as emerging spiritually above his own psychophysical condition, and this is the existential act. " By this very act man enters the spiritual dimension of being, nay, he even creates this dimension as a dimension of its own. Man begins to behave as man only as soon as he proves to be able to move within the spiritual dimension." [27]

The task of working on the problem of an adequate concept of man is the more challenging in view of the implications of the "object" idea prevalent in the political thinking of our day. There are plenty of threatening forces willing to reduce man to an object, and should this way of life prevail, science itself would inevitably be stultified. Frankl has reiterated that the ultimate responsibility for the Nazi gas chambers lies not in a decision in Hitler's chancellory but in unexamined nihilistic philosophies of university lecture halls that fail to give adequate answer to the question: Who is man? The idea that human beings can be gassed to death because they are considered of no further use to a perverted society is revolting even to those far removed from the horrors of war. But it is revolting only because even in unthinking folk there lurks the idea of man that invests him with dignity and value. Psychotherapy accordingly has the profound responsibility of delving still deeper into the nature of man than it yet has been able to do.

Chapter III

Concept and Status of Man
in Psychotherapy

1. Anthropology in Naturalistic Psychotherapy

Alexander Pope told his fellow man two hundred years ago,
"The proper study of mankind is man," but man still remains
his own most disturbing problem. The years since Pope's observation have been marked by extraordinary advances in the
understanding of nature, but this is matched by a cacophony
of confusion in the understanding of man. Concepts of man
range all the way from the mechanical ideal of the thinking
machine, through the assertion of naturalistic humanism that
man is all the god there needs to be, to Christian anthropology.
The Christian teaching is that man rises out of nothingness by
a creative act of God. His existence and his meaning can be
understood only as they are seen related to God and to all
creation, making him thus "the measure of all *things*."

Cultural anthropology, sociology, and psychology in recent
years have amassed vast quantities of data on man, but there
is little cross-fertilization to bring about the flowering of this
knowledge. Max Scheler has described the situation pointedly:
"We possess a scientific, philosophical, and theological anthropology that care nothing about each other. But we do not
possess a unified concept of man." [1] It is urgently obvious that
only through co-operation of all who work with man and his
relationships can the knowledge and insights on human nature
now accumulating be best applied to human problems. The
unhappy coinage of the term "human engineering" demon-

strates the extent to which object-thinking dominates in our present-day culture.

Two basic facts about human existence have received considerable attention in philosophical and psychological debate: One is that "man is a child of nature, subject to its vicissitudes, compelled by its necessities, driven by its impulses, and confined within the brevity of years which nature permits its varied organic form." Psychoanalytic research has operated to provide a good deal of light here. The other fact with which philosophy and religion in the past have dealt is that "man is a spirit who stands outside of nature, life, and himself, his reason and the world." [2] This second fact is particularly attractive to the modern existentialists who insist upon man's capacity for self-transcendence and his ability to make himself his own object. Even our overworked, illustrative man in the street senses this existential truth in his experience of feeling like kicking himself for something he has done. Occasionally he curiously asks himself, "What part of me judges what other part of me in this feeling?" Here is a naïve but accurate approach to self-transcendence. That man is unique and that he also is a product of nature are seemingly irreconcilable facts that are at the source of much confusion in our thinking concerning man.

The complex organization of man is basically explained in biological and developmental terms by psychoanalytically oriented writers, beginning, of course, with Sigmund Freud. Psychoanalysis was indirectly influenced by the old, dualistic, body-mind theories that conceived of man as existing in two levels — a biological-natural level and a mental-spiritual level. Suspicious of the approach from the rational upper level, analysis seeks to understand the nature of man from the bottom biological level. Even though the rational level is greatly minimized in accounting for motivation, does not an unconscious allegiance to a dualistic view of man point to a serious flaw at the beginning of the analytic approach? Again, the biological facts are simple facts that rational man may not evade, for he does share drives and impulses with the animals. Nevertheless, these still are not the same, in the wholeness of human organization, as they are in the instinctual behavior of animals. Something akin to anticipatory anxiety can be seen in animals, but animals do not build up anything like guilt feelings, remorse, or conscience. The biological approach has dredged up a lot of knowledge of man, but it gives no insight into the origin of more complex phenomena such as freedom. An illumination of this can be seen in Freud's own honest explanation of his change of view on the Oedipus complex: "To our astonishment, the result was the reverse of what we had expected. It is not repression that creates anxiety; it is there first and creates repression." [3] Perhaps man's freedom of choice and its misuse creates the anxiety, for Freud discounts the birth-trauma idea of Otto Rank,[4] who found the source of anxiety in the act of birth. Freud takes a more conservative view than Rank's, writing: "Intrauterine life and early infancy form a continuum to a far greater extent than the striking caesura of the act of birth would lead us to believe." [5]

Man's unconscious impulses are found in the strata of the id, which seeks satisfactions for its drives (*Triebe*), according to the pleasure principle. There is little organization within the id, whose impulses run riot, and have been described in terms like "anarchy" and "chaos," but the sexual drive is basic, in lead of the others in demanding expression. Knowledge of the true nature of the id comes from the interpretation of dreams. However, dreams also contain much that is not reducible to mere biological impulses unless, as Niebuhr jokingly says, it can be "supposed that animals are troubled by the Oedipus complex and suffer from a guilty conscience because incestuous impulses struggle for expression in the depths of their unconscious." [6] Dreams also use symbols and ideas, images that are constructs of man's rational nature, and which are thus called upon or used in analysis to understand the deep, irrational contents of the unconscious area.

An appreciation of changes in emphasis that have come

about in analytic terminology may be helpful to pastors and counselors. The concept of unconscious mental functioning is one of Freud's great contributions, but is the word "unconscious" to be used as an adjective or a noun? Freud's early discussions gave the connotation of the unconscious as a place where the instincts are located. It is generally used today as an adjective, with no implication of location in a particular place. The same difficulty attends the use of the term "id." The distinction between the unconscious and the id has not yet been clearly made by analytic workers. The id, though, is generally conceded to be illogical, amoral, and purposeless. It seeks to gratify libidinal urges and thus becomes a reservoir of libido since it is the source of instinctual energy in man. Freud ultimately classified the instincts into two categories: the life instinct (Eros), which included libido and some of the ego instincts, and the death instinct (Thanatos), based on the tendency of organic life to return to previous inorganic conditions. The unconscious, in addition to instincts, covers a great area of mental life including conscious material that has been repressed, or material that never came to consciousness. The dynamic nature of the unconscious is seen in its profound capacity to affect emotional life, rational life as well as organic states, since its impulses seek expression in every possible way. The conscious mind, of course, is unaware of this subtle, ongoing activity. Gerald S. Blum's systematic review of psychoanalytic theories of personality [7] is an interesting discussion of variations in interpretation and application of Freudian theory, and a particularly helpful contribution of the neo-orthodox school is Clara Thompson's discussion of psychoanalysis as related to evolution and development.[8]

The id, as the deepest part of the psyche, is not in contact with the world but only with the body, and there it is dominated by the *pleasure principle.* The ego, as the second level of development, begins to form as the infant begins to make distinctions between self and the world of objects. In contrast to the id, then, the ego is in touch with reality through perception and thought. The *reality principle* means the capacity of reacting to the demands of the environment, and adjusting behavior accordingly. This becomes part of the ego structure and it tends to modify or replace the pleasure principle. Some writers, again, do not differentiate id and ego, perferring to speak of id-ego. The superego is differentiated still later and develops from the parental standards and the moral standards of society as these are perceived by the ego. It is considered to be divided into two parts, the ego ideal and the conscience. The ego has to establish some sort of harmony between the demands of the superego and the wild impulses of the id. In addition to outside standards the superego also includes personal ideals and the capacity for self-criticism. Fromm identifies the authoritarian conscience, the voice of internalized external authority, with the superego.[9] The fascinating list of defense mechanisms — the " vocabulary of defeat " — their description, their clinical and analytic treatment, all stem from the actions and relations of the id, ego, and superego, as well as the interrelationship of these with the external world and society.

Freud felt that the successes in the therapy of psychoanalysis are proof of the validity of the theory. Blum, however, is willing to debate the matter for two reasons: " First of all, we have no good evidence yet regarding a greater proportion of cures by psychoanalytic treatment than by any other methods; and secondly, there is no way to determine, even in an eminently successful case, how much and in what ways the therapist's theoretical orientation contributed to the complex interpersonal relationship which resulted in the patient's improvement." [10] The question of validity of theory can be left to the medical historian, but it is obvious that variations which have developed in the application of analytic theory show the concern of the therapist for the mystery and subtlety of conflicting elements and forces within man. This concern, entirely apart from the validity of the theory, helps to establish the successful relationship that earlier was emphasized as the common ground of healing potential in all schools.

A different approach has found a source of neurosis in the learning process. Dollard and Miller,[11] working with the theory that measurable traits of the normal personality can be traced to the learning process, surmised that the neurotic personality is learned. The insight that educational influences in human development can cause neurosis is well supported in their research. Anxiety, then, which Freud found to be, not the result of repression, but its cause, and not the result of birth trauma, can be learned. Here the existentialists — of any school — in their insistence upon freedom, provide a corrective to naturalistic and deterministic ways of thinking and proceeding. Anxiety is closely related to human freedom, to its misuse, or failure to measure up to the necessity of assuming responsibility that is inherent in the concept and fact of freedom. The capacity of the id for outwitting the watchful eye of the ego and its censoring proclivity is described in detail in analytic writings. But this capacity cannot itself be explained merely in biological terms, even though, as Freud maintains, there are areas of the ego and the superego that also are unconscious.[12] This capacity of the id to outwit the ego is a form of freedom, though admittedly a simple or low level, and it indicates that there is more in the nature of man, something above and beyond nature, than can be accounted for by drives shared with the animal world.

The fact of history and its relevance to the nature of man lends further urgency to the need of formulating a more adequate concept. Man is a product of nature; but he has creative capacity that, if it is not used or directed constructively, produces neurosis and anxiety in individuals and chaotic relations among nations. *Man makes history* by his responsible (and irresponsible) acts, by how he uses his creative gifts. If he is to be explained solely by nature and biology, then history is unexplained or meaningless because nature, when the free decisions of responsible persons are excluded, is simply a process of change.

Due to inherent difficulties in the problem itself as well as to the many variants in theory, no unified concept of man, his internal structure, character, self, or personality is to be found in psychoanalytic theory. Gerald Blum, winnowing two hundred ninety-five books and publications of analysts of several shades of thought, concludes his book with the forthright admission that it presents a confused picture. "It seems as though a large number of psychoanalysts through many years of observing patients, discussing cases, and borrowing from their own unconscious ideas have contributed to a massive, vague, yet potent personality theory. Encompassed are many controversial issues and many sharp disagreements." [13] To Blum's evaluation can be added the observation that there is also a great deal of overlapping and some needless semantic circumnavigation around the same basic ideas.

Despite the lack of cohesive concepts of man's nature, psychoanalysis recognizes an internal character structure of the self that is not entirely determined by drives and unconscious forces. Inherited disposition and the influences of the environment enter into this structure, but the self that results also develops a kind of unity that relates both passively and actively to the environment of things and people. Karen Horney has aided understanding of neurosis at this point with her description of three basic attitudes or character types: those who are moving toward, moving against, and moving away from people.[14] These are the compliant type, the aggressive type, and the detached type. They overlap in some areas the introversion-extroversion types of Jung as well as the typologies of Spranger, Rank, Fromm, Sheldon, and others. The clarity of her description and style, however, gives no grounds for complaint as to ambiguity or special vocabulary. Ernst Kretschmer's work on the relationship of body build and personality or character is well known,[15] and Sheldon's work in morphological types is attacking the problems of typology systematically with a long-range program of investigation.[16] Though it has interesting phases, not much help for therapy can be expected from typological investigations and formulas.

It is no mystery that a clearly worked out definition of the self, aware of its uniqueness, is difficult to achieve. Some of the contents of unconscious states have been thoroughly explored, but the work has only begun even here. Analysis seems to be content with aiding the self in its striving to attain equilibrium with regard to the often dismaying inner world and the tough demands of the external world.[17] The criticism so easily thrown at adjustment psychology can be made here too. If adjustment is the goal, what about external conditions or cultures to which the patient is to be adjusted? If the culture is sicker than the patient, what is the responsibility of the therapist? Biography and history and culture itself contain many reminders that much creative work is done by people who have refused to adjust to their world as they found it. Freud's own monumental contributions come in significant part from his and his patient's reactions to Viennese culture. The progress of science has been marked both by the contributions of the intuitive workers with their flashes of insight, and by the plodding, most necessary work of the systematic approach. No one would seriously urge the intuitively gifted scientist to pay no heed to his intuitions in favor of adjustment to the more exact approach of experiment and measurement. This might rule out the possibility of achievements like those of Newton, whose three great discoveries came within a period of two years. The history of scientific investigation shows many cases similar to Newton's achievements, and it would seem that intuition lies at the roots of any science, from mathematical axioms to the natural sciences.[18]

A very warm appreciation of the contribution of psychoanalysis to man's self-understanding was written by the late Prof. David E. Roberts. But he also sharpens the issue as to the importance of the ultimate concept of man in this way: "Psychotherapy is one version of modern psychology which cannot get along wthout the 'psyche.' It sees physical, biological, and unconscious processes as participating in the life of a self which is held together, in the end, by consciousness and purposiveness. Indeed, unless the therapist believed that conscious intention can influence events, he could not carry on his work at all. Because psychotherapy is committed to the increase of man's capacity to achieve responsibility, it must oppose those forms of psychology which, when taken seriously, spread the illusion that man is an automaton." [19] This thought of Professor Roberts' is further elaborated in connection with the teachings of Christian theology on freedom and determinism. He, along with Professor Tillich, has done pioneer work in relating therapy and religious thought concerning the nature of man. I am convinced that even as therapy stands to gain by shaping its ideas of man so also Christian theology needs to overhaul its doctrine of man, in the interests of helping him to "be transformed by the renewal of his mind."

Whether practitioners of various schools in psychotherapy can agree with the idea that purposiveness and intention are vital to a self-concept will depend not only on their philosophical outlook but also on the extent to which that outlook is a conscious force in therapy. Freud was influenced to a significant extent, as was the rest of his generation, by Nietzsche, whose existentialism was perverted into a nihilism that is under the fire of existentialists in both philosophy and psychology. In America two generations have grown up in a technical society that has relegated philosophy to the back wards of a sick civilization. To them, Nietzsche is just a name, and philosophy a luxury easily dispensed with in the hard necessity of acquiring all the vast array of facts and techniques required for a medical, a psychological, or a sociological education.

If an immature *Weltanschauung* is not disciplined by some formal philosophy, it subsides into an unconscious but none the less powerful influence. The extent to which psychotherapists are deterministic in their outlook may well shape their view of man as an automaton, an object to be manipulated and adjusted to its best possible function in whatever society happens to prevail. Here the possibilities open to "industrial

psychology " and " human engineering " are enough to give a
sensitive scientist nightmares. If determinism and adjustment
to a particular society (as society in turn is determined by the
culture of which it is a part) are to be in the philosophical
background or unconscious of psychotherapy, then the concept of man will always be relative to the culture.

Prophets of all the great religions always have challenged
the culture of their day, and so have the intuitive workers in
science who repeatedly upset " empiric facts." An example of
this is Max Planck's quantum of action h that had the implication that Heisenberg expressed in his " Uncertainty Principle."
This states that " a particle can have a position or it can have
a velocity, but in the strict sense it cannot have both. Nature
puts up with our probings into its mysteries only on conditions.
The more we clarify the secret of position, the more deeply
hidden becomes the secret of velocity. It reminds one of the
man and woman in the weather house: if one comes out, the
other goes in. The product of the two unknowns is always an
integral multiple of an elementary quantum of action. We can
distribute the uncertainty as we wish, but we can never get
away from it." [20] The experimental work with this principle
of Heisenberg on the activities of photons so impressed Arthur
Compton that he saw in it serious implications for our thought
on man's freedom, and so he addressed himself to this problem in his Terry Lectures at Yale.[21]

A time when the physicist is concerned with quantum action
almost to the point of reverence (i.e., Heisenberg's stress upon
mystery) is certainly no time for therapy to solve the question
of the mystery of man by deciding that he is an object that
can be manipulated in a world where the photon yet remains
" free "! Such a decision can use determinism and relativism
not only to stifle man's potential development, but it will suf-
focate science itself under the totalitarian blanket. Analysts
in a totalitarian regime will adjust patients to subservience
under party leaders, and if the regime rules that Rankian analysis should supplant orthodox Freudian analysis, what then?

As yet totalitarianism has not completely stifled the conscience. Frankl reports that analysts in totalitarian countries have a category, "party functionary's disease," which results when a man's decency rebels against the necessity of carrying out party orders.

A basic problem for determinisms of all kinds is to account for, or to encourage, responsibility. The history of theology is replete with wordy debates on predestination (a religious term for a kind of determinism) and human responsibility or free will. It is only fair to the facts to assert that many arguments both by protagonists and antagonists tend to present predestination (which in Biblical truth always involves the purpose of a personal, loving Spirit) in the caricature of a blind, impersonal fatalism. Neither philosophy nor religion have yet adequately encompassed the problem, and it may well be that, like Heisenberg's Principle, we may evade it or ridicule it, but "we can never get away from it." An honest and scientific therapy also will neither evade nor ridicule, for already it knows too much about man to make light of his still deeper mysteries.

The evasion of responsibility on the part of the patient often is a central difficulty for the therapist to handle. The chaos of the id requires such strenuous expenditure of energy as the superego attempts to control chaotic forces — not to mention the guidance of the therapist — that the ego is somehow lost in the conflict. It is no wonder that neurosis becomes a sort of uneasy equilibrium that enables the patient to function in society. If guilt for the id impulses, and also anxiety for failure to measure up to superego requirements, fill a man's life of day-to-day existence, then there is literally no time left for the development of a responsibility or morality that is the result of the free choices of the individual. He becomes driven by inner compulsions and a feeble effort to do what "they" out there in society expect him to do. It follows that therapy faces here a central interest of religion: the freeing of man from the egocentric circle of self-love, with its inevitable disillusionment, to the wide perspective of membership in an ultimately universal society guided by the "law within" and not merely by external compulsion. Frankl argues this point: "No one should be surprised today that young people so often behave as if they did not know anything about responsibility, option, choice, sacrifice, self-devotion, dedication to a higher goal in life, and the like. Parents and teachers, scientists and philosophers, have taught them all too long a time that man is 'nothing but' the resultant of a parallelogram of inner drives and outer forces. Again and again I am reminded of the Psalter where we find a verse running like this: 'The idolizers became like the idols they were worshipping.' In actual fact man becomes more and more like the image of the man he has been taught about. Man grows according to his interpretation of himself."

Naturalistic psychotherapy, if it is to reach man in his mystery as well as in his manifold weaknesses, is under the necessity of formulating a concept of man that includes more than individual conditioning and cultural influences, important as these admittedly are. The neurotic, impulse-driven, conflict-ridden man of the couch obviously is not the norm, any more than were the bored patients of Freud's nineteenth-century Vienna, despite the vast amount of knowledge gleaned from these. Pathology has always taught that the abnormal states throw light upon normal being, even as a photographic enlargement brings out obscure details. Nor is the average man in the street in the "gray-flannel suit" the norm despite the fact that he may seem to live above his problems without either solving them nor yet failing to function socially.

A human norm that can be closely related to the continuous growth of the empiric sciences of man needs to be universally valid. In the absence of such an implicit or explicit norm there can often take place the projection of the therapist's own personal goals or preferences in the world of values. Every therapist is aware of the possible danger of using a patient for his own needs or ends, a danger to be guarded against in theory

as much as in consultation-room attitudes. Can the transcendent mystery of quantum physics again serve here as an analogy
for the similar and tantalizing mystery of man, or is man the
creature who can lift himself by his own bootstraps? Can humanistic therapy face the problem of the concept of man in-
tensively enough to face also what Heidegger has called " the
idea of transcendence, namely, that man is something which
reaches beyond itself, that he is more than a rational creature "? [22] Psychoanalysis opened the eyes of twentieth-century
man to irrational elements in his nature as well as the soft but
persistent voice of reason. This has undoubtedly worked as an
effective counterbalance against a too confident emphasis upon
rationalism. But now we have psychologies with no interest in
the psyche, or the self, and we have known men who use the
mind to doubt its existence. A little strychnine is good for certain heart ailments, but a little more than a little will stop the
heart permanently! Perhaps continuing research into the unconscious nature of man will uncover not only the anxiety all men
know but also a transcendent thirst for eternal values that ante-
dates childish aggression against pathetic patterns of conform-
ity dictated by anxious and unwise parents or churches!

Naturalistic humanism as anthropology should eventually see
that the obvious fact that man transcends nature also is not isolated from the fact that man transcends himself in choosing and
deciding. If it cannot see this, then its philosophy was written
for it by Nietzsche, whose work was interpreted by many to
mean that life is ultimately meaningless, that nature, " red in
tooth and claw," tells the full and only story of man.

It is only fair to urge that profound existentialist elements of
Nietzsche's philosophy were overlooked when his concept of
the will to power was seized upon as a vindication of egocen-
tricity and brutality. He intended it to include man's self-disci-
pline, and then his creative and artistic mastery of his environment, of the earth. Matching Nietzsche's sincere conviction that
" God is dead " was his awareness of the tragedy lurking in this
kind of world where man, cut off from the Being of God, stands

alone. Here too is some of the existential source of Sartre's
"nothingness." If God is dead, man is pushed by necessity to
tasks of creating values, of self-realization, of self-affirmation.
In contrast to Nietzsche's thought, the living God of Christianity does not push but pulls or appeals to man with transcendental values that come into history and have left an ineradi-
cable mark there. The low level of Christian influence in world
affairs today indicates that Nietzsche has accurately delineated
the ethos of our age and the principle that dominates too heavily in human concerns. A world of nothingness without, and the
emptiness of man within, present him with that "dreadful freedom" which is his to use in creating a new man and a new
world. The clever alliteration of "the age of anxiety" does not
blind the existentialist to the necessity of a profound consideration of the depths of need in human nature.

If men are but objects, as scientific methodology increasingly
tends to use them, and also if they are only products of nature,
then a law of nature is that the strong devour the weak. Thus
there is ultimately no reason why strong nazi "supermen"
should not have disposed of the "weak" (political enemies,
Jews, intellectual recalcitrants) in their concentration camps,
and waged war to insure the domination of the strong. But all
this seems so familiar to those who have turned the pages of
history, even with only passing interest. Ancient Sparta practiced infanticide and war to develop strong men and went
down in devastating defeat! Athens developed the human mind
and still rules significantly there.

2. Anthropology in Existential Logotherapy

Existential analysis in the form of logotherapy urges serious
consideration of the noetic (spiritual) category, denoting a
reality with its own expression, forms, motives, and purposes.
It urges that this category must be appreciated along with the
category of the physical and natural if we are to get anywhere
in the discussion of man's nature, as well as progress in the
healing of his ills. Many of us have argued that man transcends

nature, believing that it is useless to argue that he does not. Even the fact that man is a part of nature, arises from nature, exerts great control over it, but ultimately is defeated by nature, nevertheless testifies to his transcendence, for he *knows* that this is his relationship to nature. As Jung has remarked, the psychic fact is more " real " than the physical fact, for we know of the latter only through the former. Dr. Owen has reminded the philosophers of nineteenth-century scientism, who are still about, that an organism such as man, who is capable of knowing nature, cannot be reduced to the level of nature. " That which does the knowing is not of the same order as that which is known." [23] If psychotherapy refuses to be limited to a purely naturalistic viewpoint, its view of man is bound to include transcendental elements. Kierkegaard reminds us that " we live forward but we understand backward." Psychoanalysis has helped us greatly to " understand backward," whereas religion has always proposed to help men to " live forward." Both might have a lot to offer each other in arriving at a more adequate concept of the man they deal with.

In the existential analysis of Viktor Frankl, the concept of man is explicit in the theory and implicit in all aspects of the therapy. A basic theorem is that " being human means being conscious and being responsible," for in this school consciousness and responsibility are seen as an entity that comprises the integrity of the human being. " To be," asserts Frankl, always means " to be different " from something else, from other existence. Thus all that is, has its being with reference to something else. He criticizes psychoanalysis for regarding neurosis as a limitation upon the ego qua consciousness, and the Adlerian individual psychology for regarding it as a limitation upon the ego qua sense of responsibility. Both theories are seen as one-sided in their emphasis, whereas logotherapy affirms that both consciousness and responsibleness play basic roles in the drama of existence. Depth psychology here is complemented by a " height psychology." Not only are the therapeutic probings of man's depths seen as a way to health, but also a realization of his latent values and capacities is urged as the only way to cure certain types of neuroses.

Logotherapy adds to the somatic and psychic dimensions of man a deliberate emphasis upon the third, spiritual, or as Frankl prefers to style it, noetic, dimension. Since an aim of psychotherapy should be to bring out the ultimate possibilities of the patient, this dimensional interpretation offers the patient not merely an occasion for problem-solving, or even the cure of disease, but also opportunity for him to grow so that motivation operates on ever higher levels. Criticism of the stress on spirituality in logotherapy will be tempered by recognition of the fact that this is a reaction against the overemphasis on instinctuality in man. In this school the term " spirit " (*Geist*) is taken to mean the core or nucleus of the personality. Choices and decisions, commitment and direction toward a future goal, all are prominent in the empiric technique of logotherapy, as well as in its theory. As Freud's work relates the past to the present in its therapy, Frankl relates the future to the present in helping the patient discover the meaning of his existence, and the wide range of values available for his responsible choice in enriching that meaning.

The logotherapeutic categories of value may help clarify how suffering and death are related to meaning in Frankl's thought and therapy. The psychotherapist as well as the doctor inevitably has to face the implications of what Frankl calls medical ministry, which sooner or later is concerned with the fact of unavoidable suffering, and with man's capacity to suffer. To most people the meaning of human existence is threatened by suffering and by death. This is seen by our typical reactions to the painful suffering of an elderly person. A friend relates how he stood at the bedside of a woman dying of a painful disease. Her sister, a very domineering person, was also there, and after visiting with the patient the two left her room. " This makes me lose my faith in God — to see her suffer so," said the woman grimly. " That's odd," replied my friend, " for the attitude she has in suffering makes me believe the more in God." The pa-

tient was a rare spirit who kept up a front of good cheer for the
sake of her daughter (a member of a cult that believes suffering is unreal), for she did not want to add to the sadness of her
daughter by appearing to be suffering. Our reactions to the un-
timely death of a young person, cut down in the very budding
of a life of promise, are quite normally those of dismay, anger
at God, the meaningless of it all. The mother of a twelve-year-
old, killed in an accident, cried to her pastor, " If I could only
understand it all, it might make sense! "

A sedative may temporarily help a grief-stricken person, but
if existential neurosis (such as arises out of despairing, hopeless
attitudes) develops, the doctor must cope with this as often as
the pastor, or oftener in a community where religious life is at
a low ebb. Frankl affirms that death cannot cancel out the
meaning of life. " If life is meaningful, then it is so whether it
is long or short, whether a man can live in his children or dies
childless. If the meaning of life consisted in reproduction, then
every generation would find its meaning only in the next generation. Hence, the problem of meaning would be postponed
from one generation to another but never solved. If the life of
each generation of man has no meaning, is it not likewise meaningless to perpetuate something that has no meaning! " He goes
on to urge that what is past is not lost, but rather, " stored and
saved from transitoriness." Of course time that has passed is
irrecoverable, but what has happened in that time is unassailable and inviolable. " The passing of time is therefore not thiev-
ery, but trusteeship. Any philosophy which keeps in mind the
transitoriness of existence need not be pessimistic." [24]

Though this is not the place to return to the problem of technique, it must be said here that in logotherapy the technique of
helping people faced with suffering or death does not consist
in handing out neat little pills of philosophical meaning. In one
case parents of a child found meaning in his death by founding
a summer camp for underprivileged children. This sort of thing
obviously is limited to very few people. In another case parents
were led to find the meaning in their deep suffering by a still

deeper attitude of kindness in all their relationships with other children. This, of course, can be neatly labeled sublimation, but sublimation can remain a mere word when urged as a therapeutic device. The patient strives for it as an impossible ideal, working within the neurotic circle of self-involvement, while neglecting the area of the meaning of his existence in *relationship to all other existence*. The patient who is depressed because life has nothing more to offer can sometimes be helped by the simple expedient of reversing his dilemma with the suggestion that he still has something to offer to life. Even a Mongoloid idiot lives a meaningful existence in the state hospital where his very helplessness brings out capacities of tenderness, concern, and love in certain otherwise hard-boiled attendants. Another analogy from a different frame of reference shows how meaning is therapeutic and not merely philosophical. A brilliant agnostic once rebuffed an eager young minister with the assertion that the church had nothing to offer him. He in turn was startled by the reply: " You are dead right; my church is full of bigots with little intellectual development. Right now we have nothing to offer you, but you have a lot to offer us in leadership and guidance." The agnostic accepted the challenge and soon was leading a men's organization that deepened the life of every member, though church history fails to record formally that its leader became a believer. Other schools of therapy use similar approaches, but logotherapy unabashedly affirms the spiritual or noetic dimension in its concept of man, with its concern for values, meaning, and responsibility for larger interests and relationship than those involved merely in self-realization. One could say that it implicitly asks the patient the question, Are you taking your present stage of development for a permanent value, or are you willing to keep growing?

Existential logotherapy makes a promising beginning in the matter of developing an adequate concept of man. The question of what kind of man we want to develop is relevant for all schools of therapy. It has been argued here that psychotherapy not only needs but has, if unconsciously, some kind of *Weltan-*

schauung. It needs still more to have a conscious concept of man, for, as Frankl observes, " a psychoanalyst, of all people, should realize the danger of leaving it unconscious." Often enough in the anthropologies of the past, whether psychological, sociological, or theological, what has been presented is a caricature of the image of man. Theological writers in commendable eagerness to exalt the glory of God have debased and effectively denied the Biblical teaching of man as the image of God, so that today it is necessary to return to the basic doctrine of Creation for a correction of this emphasis. No one has worked harder toward achieving a realistic reappraisal of man and his culture than Kierkegaard in theology and Sorokin in cultural anthropology. Psychoanalysis, in significant measure, is a reaction against the smug and hypocritical images of man abundant in nineteenth-century culture and religion. Certain extremes of deterministic thought, however, end with a fatalistic view of man that goes far beyond even extreme and fatalistic distortions of the Augustinian and Calvinistic idea of the predestination of man. Reinhold Niebuhr has discussed both sides of this question at length in the first volume of his Gifford lectures on man's nature and destiny.[25]

In discussing the relationship of morality to the unconscious energy of man, Jung writes: " Unfortunately there is no doubt about the fact that man is, on the whole, less good than he imagines himself or wants to be. Everyone carries a shadow, and the less it is embodied in the individual's conscious life, the blacker and denser it is." [26] Perhaps Jung is giving psychoanalytic account of the same insight that theology has tried to exposit with its doctrine of original sin and depravity of man. In explaining what he means by the shadow (it is the real part of a person, or personal experience) Jung calls attention to the fact that repressed tendencies are not always decidedly evil, for some are merely inferior, childish, and primitive. The difficulties of living with a saint, he argues, are due to the saint's complete unawareness of repressed materials in his unconscious, which come out in irritability, etc. Now if this is true of the

" saint," is it not also true of the " worldling " whose blatancy
as to values may also be a species of whistling in the dark to
avoid proddings from the unconscious concerning values?
Frankl has insisted that, in contrast to impulses and drives of
the instinctual nature, values " call " man to make choices and
decisions in accord with the responsibleness that also is part
of his being! A synthesis of the two views is approached in the
following conclusion of Jung, which is in the tradition of logotherapy: " Such problems are never solved by legislation or
tricks. They are only solved by a general change of attitude.
And the change does not begin with propaganda and mass
meetings, or with violence. It begins with a change in individuals. It will continue as a transformation of their personal likes
and dislikes, of their outlook on life and of their values, and
only the accumulation of such individual changes will produce
a collective solution." [27] Jung might have been thinking of Nazi
Germany when he wrote those words, but they strike also at
comfortable American assumptions that our forms of propaganda (advertising), violence (the integration problem), and
mass meetings (great evangelistic campaigns) can solve economic, social, and religious problems.

Though a great deal of light has been thrown by psychoanalysis on how social mores are entangled with morality in the
personality levels of id, ego, and superego relationships, yet it
is evident that morality as a value still has not been dealt with
adequately. When psychotherapy, in attempting to handle marriage problems that revolve about the inability of the neurotic
to establish genuine love relations, is tempted to prescribe mature love as a dynamic power, it runs into yet more difficulty.
One of our political platitudes goes, " Eternal vigilance is the
price of liberty," yet each generation must learn that freedom is
not inherited — it must be deserved, earned, and fought for. So
also with love, as Kierkegaard has reminded us; each generation is under the necessity of learning to love and to relate to
fellow man. The difficulty for therapy at this juncture is pointed
out by Rollo May: " This implication is particularly relevant to

psychotherapy, since the popular mind so often makes of psychoanalysis and other forms of psychotherapy the new technical authority that will take over for them the burden of learning to love." [28] Perhaps the anxiety that this gratuitous authority produces in psychotherapists accounts for some of their earnest writings on the need for love, for we all are too aware that it cannot be used as a technical device.

Love is enacted by the therapist in his attitude of acceptance and understanding of the patient. Appearing thus in a genuine form in therapy, and thereby enabling the patient to grow in awareness of its power, then therapy must face the fact that here is the most absolute of all absolutes. There is nothing higher in the realm of value than love; other values may equal it, but none can surpass it: " The greatest of these is love." Christianity, someone has said, has survived in spite of its friends more than despite its enemies, and the chief reason for this is its central conviction — God is love. One must hasten to add a corollary to avoid a pantheistic use of the above idea, for it does not also follow that all " love " is God! It remains true, however, that if man could realize his basic capacity for mature love, most mental illness would disappear. Morality no longer would appear a complex and perplexing problem for man to solve, but would be as normal and natural as physical health.

3. Body-Mind Theory and the Wholeness of Man

Psychotherapy has recognized the validity of love, and in one way or another uses it in its concept of man. Can it go farther to include other values — such as freedom, responsibility, and meaningful existence — that are employed in logotherapy? One problem that confuses discussion here is the persistence of the old Platonic dualism of body and soul. Thinkers in the Christian tradition are re-emphasizing the Biblical view of man as a unity that cannot be deftly divided into body and soul. These include Niebuhr, Tillich, Roberts, Owen, and others who are interested in rescuing man from the simple but erroneous solution that sees him as a " good " soul temporarily occupying an " evil " body of flesh. In a discussion of basic doctrine for the layman, the fact is stressed that God as Creator leaves an indelible mark of goodness upon all that he creates.[29] This still leaves us with the philosophically insoluble problem of evil, but it delivers us from the Platonic error. Nevertheless, Nygren's penetrating analysis of love in his *Agape and Eros,*[30] which contrasts the pure love of Biblical doctrine with the egoistic love doctrines of classical thought, can be warped into the Platonic error. It is sometimes interpreted to mean that *agapē* is the higher love of the soul, while *erōs* is the lower love associated with the body and its needs. So facile a separation of soul from its bodily expression cannot honestly be made, nor is it Biblical. In Genesis the myth of Adam and Eve includes the divine command to reproduce. In the New Testament (Matt. 7:11) Jesus compares human affection and love with God's, and not at all to the discredit of the former! The Bible nowhere makes a sharp contrast between natural human love and the working of divine love in man.

As long as theological writers continue to use the dualistic body-soul terminology, psychotherapists cannot be criticized for following suit. New movements within the Christian church indicate that it is ready to re-examine its doctrine of man along with other dogmas. Not only perennial ferment at the denominational level but the ecumenical interest of the World Council of Churches and of the new pope support the observation of Prof. Arnold B. Come that " the faith of the church is a living relationship with God in Jesus Christ. It is through this relationship that God moves decisively to establish his Kingdom on earth. The church's doctrinal formulations of that faith, therefore, are its attempts at ever new self-understanding as God calls it to fulfill its single perennial task of proclaiming the one and only gospel in the midst of ever new conditions." [31] He goes on to warn that the church should not be satisfied with ancient creeds in its fear of new creeds, and suggests that a new period of doctrinal ferment is at hand. His own scholarly discussion of human spirit and Holy Spirit is a profound contribution. It is to be hoped that the church will clarify its dualistic language about the nature of man, for this will be of service not only to religion but to psychotherapy. In defining the function of the psychoanalyst, for example, Erich Fromm writes: " The analyst is not a theologian or a philosopher and he does not claim competence in those fields, but as a physician of the soul he is concerned with the very same problem as philosophy and theology: the soul of man and its cure." [32]

Frequent references to the soul are made in the writings of Jung, in whose thinking the soul is greater than the ego, which is the element of consciousness. The soul on the other hand extends into or includes the unconscious. Everything to do with the soul is real, for the soul is experienceable only as life. It is perhaps relevant here to point out that in Jung's work as in German psychology in general there is no aversion to the use of the word " soul." The word in German is, of course, *Seele,* which really means " psyche," while the word *Geist* means " spirit." But *Seele* is as often translated as " soul." In assessing Jung's writings on the cure of souls in his discussion of the awareness in modern science of the problem of perception and the necessary obsession with epistemology, Hans Schaer writes: " The same problem is particularly urgent for psychology because it is knowledge of the soul, and this knowledge can come only through the soul. It demands a certain degree of consciousness to recognize the reality of the soul. We live in and through the soul and are so wrapped up in it that we do not notice it at all. It is — in the Kantian sense — a phenomenon. To recognize the difference between the thing-in-itself and the thing-as-it-appears requires a degree of psychic consciousness and differentiation which mankind reaches only quite late and which is by no means given to all even today." [33]

The above discussion should serve to point out the fact that the survival of dualistic ideas and language in the discussion of man's nature in terms of body and soul is no mere semantic affair, nor is it a result of the difficulty of translating German words such as *Seele* and *Geist*. The modern existential writers speak of " man's capacity of transcending himself," " opposing himself," and to a significant extent this is what the older writers mean by referring to man's soul. Now, if the implications of ancient dualism are clearly understood by psychological as well as by theological writers, the semantic business will be taken care of. What is more important, the way should then be paved for a synthesis of the helpful contributions toward the under-standing of man that are available today from the work of the physiological, psychological, sociological, and theological stud-ies of human nature. If ancient quarrels over terms like super-natural vs. natural, science vs. religion, and faith vs. reason can be forgotten as children forget their boasts over whose daddy is the strongest, a more helpful concept of man ought to be forthcoming than has yet been known. And this should be of profound benefit to psychotherapy and religion.

To pose the ancient quarrels in one more view: to nineteenth-century science, reality always meant a demonstrable, material " reality " capable of being tested by laboratory and experi-ment. When " soul " did not submit to test it was immediately suspect as far as " reality " was concerned, and then Watsonian behaviorism conveniently got rid of the close relative of the soul, the mind, by reducing it to stimulus-response bonds. One recalls McDougall's facetious remark: " John Watson made up his windpipe that he had no mind."

Today, not only has quantum physics broadened the older view of reality, but we have the picture of naturalistic human-ists like Fromm saying a kind word for the soul, while theolo-gians are ready to surrender the concept " soul " if by it is meant " something " that a man " has." (An excellent discussion of this problem is found in Arnold B. Come's recent book, *Human Spirit and Holy Spirit*, The Westminster Press. 1959.) With Fromm speaking of therapy as the cure of souls, Jung holding man to be a psychophysical being, Freud pointing out dark depths, and Frankl with the existentialists describing the heights of which man's nature is capable, psychotherapy should be able to come to terms with an adequate concept of man.

The Biblical view of the wholeness of man, of his unity, will provide an additional corrective to the old dualistic view.

Man in his full uniqueness, as purposive organism, can never be adequately encompassed within the descriptive confines of a rational concept. Perhaps general agreement on even a few basic essentials may never be forthcoming among therapists when we remember the many shades of differences on theory and therapy. But man himself is far more important than our theories about him, and co-operation as to a working hypothesis at least should enable us to smoke out our unconscious concepts of man. Religious anthropology has always held that the fundamental value of human existence lies within man himself. Otherwise, the meaning of his life can be destroyed by environmental forces beyond his control. "Consider your heart with all diligence, for out of it are the issues of life." "Man's life does not consist in the abundance of his possessions." "Man shall not live by bread alone." "As he thinketh in his heart, so is he." These are but a few brief statements of the way Biblical religion has taught that inner security cannot be attained by fulfilling normal desires for the things that wealth can buy, or for pleasure, power, or fame. Therapy of all kinds has also demonstrated that the deeper needs of man can be fulfilled only within man himself.

If the individual life does not have meaning, then the reproduction of ourselves is the most meaningless thing we do, according to Frankl, for it perpetuates insignificance. This is the sad conclusion of some thinkers like Clarence Darrow who was reported to have said: "Life is an unpleasant interruption of nothingness," and of Mark Twain, whose pessimism was seen in his statement: "A myriad of men are born; they labor and sweat and struggle for bread . . . they vanish from a world where they were of no consequence; where they achieved nothing; where they were a mistake and a failure and a foolishness; where they left no sign that they ever existed — a world that will lament them a day and forget them forever." [34] In optimistic contrast the stress of personalistic psychology upon *becom-*

ing ties in with Christian theology that sees man's infinite capacity of development. In this view heaven is no " pie in the sky " of the Marxian, nor yet the eternal rest home for weary laborers in the Lord's vineyard. To the contrary, it is a state of intense activity of personalities engaged in stimulating processes of eternal growth. Though this may be called a mystical intuition, it is also a logical inference of Frankl's teaching that suffering and death cannot cancel the meaning of existence.

4. Anthropology and Christian Theology

Since Christian references have been made in preceding pages with respect to values and the concept of man, a concise summary of Christian thought on man is in order here, in full awareness that no credal statements can ever be definite and final. (For a more complete treatment of the subject the reader is referred to Reinhold Niebuhr's monumental Gifford Lectures, *The Nature and Destiny of Man.*) The Christian doctrine of man begins as does the Bible with an affirmation concerning God as the Creator of all that exists, *ex nihilo.* It is boldly anthropomorphic in asserting that God is personal, self-conscious Spirit. The weakness of the anthropomorphic term of personality is evident, as it connotes our own human limitations as well as a tendency to identify person and physical body, but it is a helpful analogy, used throughout the Bible. Just as two people do not really know each other until they reveal their inmost selves to each other, so God reveals his truth and purpose to man, this self-disclosure of God reaching its climax in Jesus Christ. Creation *ex nihilo* affirms that nothing is prior to God, for he calls all existence into being without using pre-existing materials. This is the Christian answer to the dualistic concept of the Greeks who held that divine, pure mind shapes an inherently evil matter, and that man *because* he has a material body is therefore evil. The concept of Creation sees the world as good because it is God's work, and it avoids the error of viewing the mind or spirit as essentially good, and the body as essentially evil. In the Christian view, God calls into existence man as a living being. Man is created and finite existence, and emphasis is upon wholeness and unity, not upon the addition of a spirit to a body. This view of human existence affords a concept of personality as the unity of body and soul that is consistent Biblical doctrine.

Man is distinguished from all the rest of nature by unique capacities that in Christian thought are gathered up in the expression "made in the image of God." This means that man does not have to apologize for having a body with its natural limitations resulting in death. It also involves man's consciousness and ability to organize his own creativity in dealing with nature. Further, man has the capacity of self-transcendence in his self-consciousness; he can stand outside himself as well as outside his world. This, however, according to Niebuhr, results in an essential homelessness of the human spirit that is the ground of all religion: "For the self which stands outside of itself and the world cannot find the meaning of life in itself or the world. It cannot identify meaning with causality in nature; for its freedom is obviously something different from the necessary causal links of nature. Nor can it identify the principle of meaning with rationality, since it transcends its own rational processes, so that it may, for instance, ask the question whether there is a relevance between its rational forms and the recurrences and forms of nature. It is this capacity of freedom which finally prompts great cultures and philosophies to transcend rationalism and to seek for the meaning of life in an unconditioned ground of existence." [35] This " unconditioned " ground of course is God, who cannot be defined rationally, but the " cultures and philosophies " do share with Christianity its concept of man as having this capacity of self-transcendence.

The teaching of the image of God does not stop with the emphasis on the unity of man who lives in finite relation to an infinite Creator. The image is in definite ways distorted by man's sin. His essence is his freedom, but he uses this freedom to sin, to assert himself in rebellion against God, to refuse to admit his creaturehood, to put self in the center of the universe, and ultimately to worship self and its desires, to honor the creature rather than the Creator. A remark of Frankl's is apropos here: " It is interesting to note that the historical moment of transformation from a geocentric astronomy to a heliocentric one coincided with the historical moment of transformation from a theocentric to an anthropocentric philosophy. The Copernican cosmogony must have caused a severe concussion in the self-appreciation of mankind, a planetarian feeling of inferiority which demanded its overcompensation. Man felt himself thrown out of the center of the cosmos, and so he set himself up at the center of being, that is, in the place of God." [36]

Two basic elements are equally stressed in Christian theology in its doctrine of man. First, his creation in the image of God affirms that man and his unique capacities are good; second, his sin that, according to the doctrine of original sin, leads him to use his capacities in the wrong way, sinfully. The first of these propositions is attractive; the second is quickly rejected by the man who is not ready for self-acceptance, though I must admit many people have been alienated by the dogmatic and arbitrary way in which the doctrine sometimes is taught. Indeed, the bitterness of some debates on sin can only be accounted for in analytic terms of the projection of our own inner conflicts onto the opponent or the doctrine! Though the doctrine seems repulsive to many, it has remarkable similarities with psychoanalytic descriptions of some neuroses: the individual is ridden by inner conflicts; he is unable to make right choices or any decisions; aggression, envy, and self-pity mark his social relations; he is so concerned with self, not only in fantasy, but in social relations that most actions of others are misinterpreted. His self-love so consumes his capacity for love that he has little left for others. Ultimately he cannot help himself. He needs a transforming power from outside, mediated to him through another personality in the relationship of therapy. If this is a fair description of some neurotic states, is it vitally different from Paul's succinct description of sin: " Worshiped and served the creature rather than the Creator "? However, the conclusion that only neurotics are sinners must not be drawn from this comparison!

The insights of psychotherapy that have resulted in significant part from a deeper knowledge of inner conflicts, can be constructively appropriated by theology to achieve a better understanding and expression of its own deep insight of original sin as misuse of freedom. It was Kierkegaard who said, " Anxiety is the dizziness of freedom." The present-day concern of existential logotherapy with relating freedom to the search for meaning and acceptance of responsibility can also operate to the advantage of both psychotherapy and theology as they deal with anxiety. The concept of therapeutic relationship (based upon genuine acceptance and understanding), which was discussed earlier, offers a suggestion for a better understanding of how the transforming power of God, acting upon the personality from without, achieves release from the power of sin that keeps man in a continual state of civil war within his inmost being. The permissive atmosphere of trust, without which therapy fails to win more than surface changes, comes close to the Christian understanding of the meaning of faith. In the Bible, faith is never belief in a prescribed number of propositions, but rather a matter of commitment, loyalty, and unreserved trust in God. Thus there is no paradox in the statement of the man who said to Christ: " I believe; help my unbelief! " if we recast his words in some such way as; " I swear to be loyal; help me when disloyalty tempts me," or as: " I want to follow your way of life. Help me when I am attracted by detours! "

In relating meaning and human misery, Frankl holds that " there is no reason to doubt the meaning of even the most miserable life. Every life, in every situation, retains a meaning to the last breath. This is just as true in the life of a psychotic person. Even the trappings of psychosis conceal a real, spiritual person, and the nucleus of man is unassailable by mental disease, indestructible, although his means of communication with the outside world are inhibited by disease. If this were not the case, it would be futile to be a psychiatrist." [37] This is but another way of stating the worth of the individual self and respect for personality that, it is generally agreed, stem from the Judaeo-Christian ethic and ethos. If man has intrinsic worth, that worth did not come from nature: he has value as a creature only because of relationship to a Creator. When a totalitarian state cynically uses man as a thing, as a machine, it is careful first to cut the silver cord that binds man to God, and then it proceeds to deify itself.

Is the transforming power released in therapy, with resultant growth and sometimes startling change in the patient merely a mundane affair, neatly explainable by our precise categories, or does it have another reference? Carl Rogers describes one aspect of therapy as follows: "When there is this complete unity, singleness, fullness of experiencing in the relationship, then it acquires the out-of-this-world quality which many therapists have remarked upon, a sort of trancelike feeling in the relationship from which both client and I emerge at the end of the hour, as if from a deep well or tunnel. In these moments there is, to borrow Buber's phrase, a real I-Thou relationship, a timeless living in the experience which is *between* the client and me. It is at the opposite pole of seeing the client, or myself, as an object. It is the height of personal subjectivity." [38] Now to jump back a couple of thousand years in the cure of souls — the conversations of Jesus with individuals, though most of them are but brief records, seem to demonstrate the quality of relationship Rogers describes, and which results in healing through insight into the distorted relationships and values of men. If transcendent power is released in therapy, the therapist should be more aware of its source, and the clergy should not neglect its tremendous significance for pastoral psychology.

Relationship in therapy is not a category but an experience shared by two human beings. If relationship is a common denominator of all varying schools of therapy, then a "negative" denominator could be a firm intention not to use people as things, but to see man always in his wholeness of being which cannot be understood except in relationship to other being. Some existentialists and all theologians would add " and to Other Being." The twentieth century has analyzed man, but some psychologies have all but fragmentized him. A synthesis must be effected before nuclear physics atomizes him and his civilization. " The proper study of man " will accord him the dignity of treatment as subject, not as an object. It will address him, not as it, but as " thou."

Chapter IV

Logotherapy in Culture
and Counseling

1. Psychological Background of Counseling

Psychology has collected much of its information on man by utilizing and adapting the assumptions and research methods of the physical and biological sciences. Before culture and its relevance to counseling are examined, let us review briefly some aspects of psychology that are of significance for counseling theory. Experiments with rats in a maze have thrown interesting light on the relative strengths of maternal, thirst, and sex needs, but conclusions as to how well this illuminates interpersonal relations depend somewhat on the presuppositions and enthusiasm of the experimentor. The files of any marriage counselor indicate that many sex problems are symptoms of other deeper personality difficulties. Experience is not so easily classified as rigidly controlled laboratory experimentation; it too has proved to be an important source of information on man.

Laboratory work will continue to compile impressive similarities that can be a source of valuable insights, but the Greeks anciently observed that similarities do not mean identities. Man has many functions in common with mechanical things, with the vegetable kingdom, and with animals. In all these functions, however, he acts as a human being, in another dimension, the distinctly human dimension that existential logotherapy calls noetic. Analogy with other dimensions of existence may help explain some difficulties (such as the vegetative life of an extremely regressed schizophrenic) but analogy cannot provide an organizing principle. The psychotic still retains the nucleus of personality that psychiatry strives to contact. The vast universe may impress one with the insignificance of man, but the astronomer remembers who built the telescope, and when Pascal observed that man is but a reed, he added the qualification: he is a "thinking reed." Professor Allport argues that whenever experimental psychology gets to the point of scorning mentalism, it moves over into another field, and leaves man to the more personalistic psychologies.[1]

In discussing the method of science as it relates to research in the laws of learning, Carl Rogers has pointed out the tremendous temptation here to use that method in manipulation of persons, events, and their relationships. Though this manipulation may be done in a very ethical way, such as in using the principle of repeated review to master a foreign language, it also poses the problem of the correct use of power, for knowledge is power, over men as well as over machines and events. "It is not too strong a statement to say that the growth of knowledge in the social sciences contains within itself a powerful tendency toward social control, toward control of the many by the few. An equally strong tendency is toward the weakening or destruction of the existential person. When all are regarded as objects, the subjective individual, the inner self, the person in the process of becoming, the unreflective consciousness of being, the whole inward side of living life, is weakened, devalued, or destroyed."[2] To a certain extent, a "laboratory" experiment in certain areas of the problem Rogers poses has already been run off for us in certain totalitarian economies. The effects on personality and culture are seen in a country like Czechoslovakia which used to sparkle with zest for living and creativity. Today visitors are depressed by its drabness and the listlessness and dispirited attitudes of its inhabitants.

A profound survey of social and cultural dynamics extending from the earliest forms of Western culture and civilization down to the present has been made by Pitirim Sorokin in his writings.[3] His findings here significantly complement those of existential logotherapy in individual psychology. He diagnoses the sickness of our present culture in a way to show that the whole culture suffers from the same tendency that Rogers sees as a deleterious influence on therapy. Since the Renaissance, states Sorokin, our culture has increasingly become sensate, that is, it has focused predominately upon sensory experience and values that can be measured only by the senses, empirically. Though this has resulted in extraordinary progress and dissemination of the arts and sciences on a scale never before attained in history, it has brought us to the impasse represented in civilization today, where our most thoughtful minds fear the possible annihilation of culture and the race as well. Sorokin pleads passionately for a return to the important elements of the ideational cultures of the past with their allegiance to spiritual and transcendent values. Though his judgments have impressed some as too severe, and his remedies as too naïve, his deep insights nevertheless are of extraordinary importance in this present era of history.

The psychotherapist is, of course, not a specialist either in sociology or culture, but indirectly, and often enough directly, almost everything he does in therapy impinges upon culture with implied if not explicit value judgments. The men he deals with are products of culture as well as products of nature, and cultural values are of concern in therapy in one way or another. And as Rogers asks, " Doesn't all this point to the fact that ethics is a more basic consideration than science? " — in order to prevent science from becoming the juggernaut that may crush rather than create. Science necessarily blocks off certain areas or levels of man for specific purposes, just as the surgeon ties off arteries and sets up other blocks in the organism of the patient to facilitate a given operation. Then the surgeon reconnects the arteries, sutures the severed tissues in the necessary interests of the patient's wholeness and health. Social scientists and therapists, who in some aspects of their work may treat man " as if " he were an animal, a bundle of reflexes, a machine, or a being with immature values, or with a magical religion, must not forget the psychic parallel of the surgeon's completion of his operative technique. For research, it may have tremendous value for knowledge to treat man as a statistic, a thinking machine, or any other kind of object; but if this treatment obscures the unique wholeness of men, than we do not end our social surgery with a whole man or an understanding of living being. We may just produce a zombi, the living cadaver of an automaton of which the rigid conformists of the iron curtain satellites may be the forerunners!

The logotherapeutic school of existential analysis, in common with the personalistic psychologies, views man as an intelligent being with a distinctive organization. Despite hereditary disposition, early conditioning, and cultural restrictions, man has a unique capacity for making choices of action, setting up purposes or goals for himself that among other things can settle conflicts of motives. This unique capacity is a form of self-determination whereby man continually decides what he is becoming in the next moment. In psychotherapy it is an accepted maxim that no client can be helped unless he really wants and is enabled to accept the necessary help to get well. This " existential maxim " is also structured in the procedure of the members of Alcoholics Anonymous who normally refuse to go to the aid of someone on the plea of a relative or friend. They assume responsibility for helping him only on the basis of treating him, even in his extreme weakness, as responsible for his actions. Where other forms of psychotherapy have failed with certain individuals, the work of Alcoholics Anonymous has succeeded in rehabilitating these men. As in all forms of therapy, the client must be willing to act in ways that point to, and ultimately result in, the recognition of goals and the resultant reorganization of personality.

The concern of existential logotherapy with meaning, responsibility, and values is important not only to counseling but to our culture and its values. Man's creativity has a bearing, not only upon the satisfactions and meaning he finds in creativity, but also upon the culture that he thereby molds and that in turn shapes him. The emphasis of the modern spirit upon the relativity of human knowledge has resulted in the growth of skepticism and irresponsibility, and the appearance of new political fanaticisms which really are forms of religion. The prevalence of *relativity, irresponsibility, skepticism,* and *fanaticism* (which might be styled the negative values that have replaced the absolute values of the former culture) has a direct bearing upon the anxiety and difficulties of the man we meet in therapy. These four negative values lead him to that existentialist abyss of meaninglessness from which he shrinks back, and his resultant reaction is anxiety. The easy faith in progress that once seemed an automatic result of the tremendous growth in scientific achievement has been shaken by recent history. Cultural history shows that the human community grows in complexity as well as in extent, even as an individual develops. The remotest parts of the world are reached by modern communications in seconds, by modern weapons in minutes, by modern transportation in hours. This amazing advance threatens to destroy civilization because our extraordinary technological progress is not matched by growth in man's capacity or desire for its altruistic use. Here it would seem that counseling therapy has not only an individual reference but also a cultural responsibility in its work of helping man realize his potentialities.

2. The Relevance of Culture and Counseling

The fall of civilizations, according to Arnold Toynbee, is not due to having reached a crest from which they naturally decline. Their failure is due to a misuse of the freedom to which their achievements have brought them, and to repressive rule by a dominant minority. Creativity in culture becomes focused upon contingent values, holding them as absolute: this confusion is a result of the idolization of an ephemeral self, as well as of " an ephemeral technique." The satire of the " solid-gold Cadillac " reminds us that the values of comfort, ease, wealth, position, power — those things that appeal to the senses — are continually before our eyes in Western culture. These values are not a unifying force in culture, if for no other reason than the competition of man in order to get them. There are not enough of these sensate values, as Sorokin calls them, to go around. Only the few can hold wealth, exercise power, or wallow in ease. However, it is not just competition for the scarce items that causes crisis. The real demon is the major principle of sensate culture: that true reality and value is sensory, that only what we perceive with the senses and subject to empiric tests is real and of value. Anything beyond this type of experience, since we cannot test it with the senses, can be ignored or assumed to have no existence. As we saw earlier, empiricism inevitably has its influence upon man in his evaluation and/or devaluation of himself. When sensate values become prominent in civilization, to the exclusion of idealistic and ideational elements, then that civilization becomes decadent because of the inevitable disintegration of the sensate form of culture.

The predominant influence of the sensate idea in much psychological work of the recent past is obvious. The difficulty this creates in formulating adequate concepts of man was discussed in Chapter III. Now that psychology has also turned its attention to cultural anthropology for better understanding of man, it should be recognized that personal problems dealt with in counseling not only are the result of individual conflicts and failures in interpersonal relationships but also of deep, extensive, cultural influences. Man has a sociocultural ego as well as a Freudian id-influenced ego. A great deal of profound thought has gone into the analysis of history, culture, and civilization on the part of men like Spengler, Toynbee, Sorokin, and Niebuhr. Freud also devoted considerable thought to culture in his work. Of these, Prof. Harry Elmer Barnes has called Toynbee and Sorokin "the twin Augustines of our era." Psychology has learned a lot from the individual work of Freud and Adler, and also from the research of Margaret Mead and other anthropologists. Since phenomenological and existential philosophy pay serious attention to the problem of values, the contributions of workers in the area of cultural values promise to provide additional insight for workers in psychology and therapy.

The relevance of Sorokin's indictment of the present era to practical problems faced in counseling is seen, for example, in the unsettled and disturbed mind of the late adolescent. Today he faces the usual necessity of vocational and educational decisions, to which now is added compulsory military training for which he has no enthusiasm and little understanding. It is seen in the apathy of many college students, whatever their major field, who study under the predominant influence of a necessarily sensate, technological science. Their religious values, often enough childishly immature or magical, are easily exposed as ridiculous by brilliant, agnostic teachers who in turn have long since relinquished their own immature religious ideology and substituted for it a devotion to scientific principle. The student has little time or inclination to develop mature experience in religious values, and still less time for philosophical discipline. His familial relationships usually are weak in a culture that has relativized the marriage bond, and whose overorganized society competes with many activities formerly centered in the family. The schools rise to this challenge by providing splendid courses on marriage and family life, but even here the experts maintain that the best education for marriage is the family and the happy home with mature parents. A side effect of the basic presupposition of determinism (itself a sensate value) is pointed out in the words of H. McArthur who "traces the apathy among students which is today so frequently noted to the complete determinism which is implied or made explicit in the teaching of the various sciences. . . . 'Choice,' 'freedom,' and 'imagination' are coming to be thought of as toys that the educated man can no longer take seriously. This is a tragic distortion of experience." [4] Every teacher who has tried to stimulate imaginative thinking in an unresponsive class understands this form of apathy.

Despite his surgical exposure of pathological tissues in our present civilization and culture, Sorokin is not pessimistic in his outlook. Though Spengler comes to pessimistic conclusions because he equates culture with natural processes, which by law grow old and die, Sorokin is optimistic. With Toynbee he rejects the analogy that the failure of civilizations is a result of the natural cycle of birth, development, and death. Toynbee holds that civilizations fall because they do not adapt to the requirements of increasingly complex conditions of life as they develop, and thus they make tragic mistakes that result in downfall.[5] The counselor well knows how the simple ethic of the typical Western movie, the " good " men versus the " bad " men, prevails in the thinking of many, and is projected into the international scene by the pathetic idea that if Russia were impotent, war no longer would be a problem. An older generation fatuously thought peace was established by eliminating the German kaiser. The international tensions of our day present us with tremendous opportunities as well as frightening possibilities, but they are but enlargements of national, communal, and individual tensions that give rise to the difficulties and anxieties that psychotherapy handles. Sorokin might agree that therapy can only be palliative until the central emphasis or major premise of our culture is honestly faced and changed. It is because I believe that counseling, in the light of the existential or logotherapeutic stress on values, can have marked influence in bringing about this change that I am urging a serious consideration of the relevance of culture to counseling.

All the great unified systems of culture, Sorokin maintains, on the basis of profoundly extensive research into the cultures of the past three thousand years [6] have been *ideational*. By this he means: " Any great culture, instead of being a mere dumping ground of a multitude of diverse cultural phenomena, existing side by side and unrelated to one another, represents a unity or individuality whose parts are permeated by the same fundamental principle and articulate the same basic value. The dominant part of the fine arts and science of such a unified culture, of its philosophy and religion, of its ethics and law, of its main forms of social, economic, and political organization, of most of its mores and manners, of its way of life and mentality, all articulate, each in its own way, this basic principle and value. This value serves as its major premise and foundation." [7] The major principle is God whom Sorokin calls "the true-reality value." His illustration for Western culture is the medieval period whose architecture and sculpture were the "Bible in stone," and whose painting, music, literature, philosophy, were predominantly religious and Christian. Its science, political organization, economic practices, social groupings, and dominant mores all were based upon God as an infinite, supersensory, and superrational God. He also holds that the integrated culture of Brahmanic India, the Buddhist and Taoist cultures, and the Greek culture from the eighth to the sixth century, B.C., were predominantly ideational.

The decline of medieval culture was simultaneous with the weakening of the ideational element that was gradually replaced by the sensate principle. In between the two systems is a blended form of culture, which Sorokin calls *idealistic*, that is partly sensate while retaining some ideational values. Since the Renaissance period, Western culture has been primarily sensory, and though it has brought extraordinary achievements to the world, the end result has been a matching, extraordinary impasse which faces men and nations today. The cure for the sickness of sensate civilization, Sorokin finds in a return to the idealistic culture that promotes sensate values without relinquishing absolute values. In our sensory culture such "supersensory values as the Kingdom of God and the like are either denied as superstitions or rendered mere lip service. These reality-values, remnants of the medieval ideational culture, are, at best, regarded as childish fantasies. Fullness and richness of life is measured by the maximum of sensory reality-values. . . . And the greater the share of wealth, comfort, power, fame, etc., one acquires, the happier and greater one is considered to be." [8]

One expects such denunciations from the preachers of religion, but here is a prophet of culture passionately pleading for a return to absolute values as the cornerstone of civilization and the chief hope of its survival! According to him everyone, from birth to death, is molded by the ethos of present-day sensory values. "The family, the nursery school, the group of children one plays with, the elementary school, high school and college, the persons and groups one meets, the papers and books one reads, the movies and plays one attends, the business one is engaged in, all these agencies incessantly induce a person to strive to become rich, powerful, and famous. Greatness and leadership are measured in quantitative terms. If one acquires only a small share of these values, he is considered a failure and relegated to the bottom rung of the social ladder. If he refuses to fight for as large a share as possible, he is regarded as devoid of ambition, perhaps as queer, maladjusted, mentally or morally abnormal." [9] Since Sorokin wrote these words, our playwrights and novelists have diligently worked to reflect or portray the frustrations, anxieties, inadequate values, and suffering of modern man, infected with the sickness of a civilization that does not see its values clearly, but none of the writers have discovered the source of the infection or come up with an antibiotic.

In vindication of the Freudian finding that egoistic individuals and groups are produced by deep conflicts and unsatisfied drives, Sorokin sets the idea that the relative paucity of sensory values (since so few really can become rich and powerful) generates a relentless and often ferocious struggle. The battle within the individual to attain his values, or the battle within groups, is not contained there but periodically breaks out into ghastly wars as nations too seek their share of the spoils, their *Lebensraum* as the Germany of World War I demanded. A sensory-minded culture thus in its very organizing principle sets up enmities among individuals, groups, and nations, and inevitably generates war while desiring peace. A group of us who were students in Germany when Hitler came to power tried to argue against militarization with the new converts to

nazism by suggesting that Germany's technological capacity
offered a way of peaceful, economic greatness. (At that time
Hitler held up the " people's car " as bait to the worker.) Our
idealistic solution or alternative was no real answer to the
dynamic difficulties that led to World War II, though today
it is ironic to view Germany's postwar prosperity, and the
omnipresence of the Volkswagen in our world!

Again with the interest of the counselor in mind as he meets
the human product of culture in his consultation room, I want
to point out a conclusion of Sorokin that bears upon our concept of man. Western culture in generating egoistic forces and
conflicts also accomplishes " the degradation of all cultural and
social values and the value of man himself to the level of mere
sensory material things." This raises the question as to what
extent the failure to deal adequately with the concept of man,
or the extent to which we are satisfied with theories that leave
man at the level of nature, are due to scientific presuppositions,
or due to the unconscious influences of our total culture. The
question is not escaped by blaming either culture or the direction it took during the Renaissance. It is settled only by facing
the choice of deciding whether or not individual man is free as
is postulated in existential logotherapy to start influencing and
changing his culture, even as that culture has influenced and
changed him and his values.

Ultimately the counselor chooses his own values, and as
Rogers has pointed out, he cannot be unconscious of those
values even though a client may perchance decide that suicide
is the solution to his difficulties. In the nondirective acceptance
of decisions, hostile feelings, and actions this acceptance involves facing the possibility of wrong or " any " choices, for
" only then does he realize the vital strength of the capacity
and potentiality of the individual for constructive action. It is
as he is willing for death to be the choice that life is chosen, for
neuroticism to be the choice that a healthy normality is chosen." [10] This dialectic will confuse only those unacquainted
with Rogers' work, and it shows how he recognizes and han-

dles moral issues in his form of therapy. One is reminded of Professor Macintosh's definition of Protestantism as an invitation to think at the level of freedom. This invitation is not without its perils, but " apart from such perils there can be no such thing as true personal faith." [11] Rogers' methodology, and Macintosh's definition both are existential!

The tendency of values in a sensory culture is to become more conditional, conventional, and increasingly relative. The culture itself is considered naturalistically and mechanistically, while man is viewed behavioristically. Widely publicized research on the sexual behavior of the human male and female leaves the deeper problems of sexual relationships to the marriage counselors, where of course they properly belong. But perhaps the number of immature marriages would not be so great if a pornographic culture did not so emphasize the value of sexual *behavior* to the neglect of the greater value of sexual *relationship.* This too could be the result of the emphasis upon technique instead of upon imagination and genuine creativity, which operate not only in artistic forms but also at one of their peaks in human interrelationships as well. It is precisely here that we have a sharp focus of neurosis: its feeling of being unloved, its inability to love and the resultant habit of using others, coercing them to fill infantile wishes with no real consideration for others, and other well-known symptoms of the neurotic failure in human relations.

Freud has taught two generations to be honest about sex. But now with typical American enthusiasm for going to extremes of having the biggest, the most, we have enthroned Aphrodite, draped, half-draped, and nude, as the goddess of the big sell. She undulates in all advertising, selling us everything from heavy machinery to pins. Sex is a real value that a behavioristic view tends to treat as an end rather than as a means to express the values of love, relationship, respect, and development of the potential of the beloved person. One view sees sex merely as a release of tension, the other as a realization of potential. In advertising, thinly disguised sex leers at us to lure us into buying the bigger and better things and thus becomes a means to the end of economic manipulation. The cultural effect of this unavoidable and ever-present stimulus, found also in books, periodicals, TV, and the theater, is to produce infantile, romantic, unreal expectations of what life is supposed to offer.[12] Invariably life slaps back with its requirement of meaningful development of potential, which, when neglected, invariably results in frustrated individuals. Instinctual drives or urges leave man poorly equipped to utilize sex in attainment of satisfaction if that satisfaction is not directly related to the values mentioned above, for, as Paul Popenoe has put it, " marriage is for adults only "! The failure of the romantic delusion to create adults is seen in the fact that psychotherapy and counseling have become " big business " that now requires licensing or other controls to eliminate quacks attracted to it. The doctor who learned to practice medicine and surgery is often exasperated by a procession of physically healthy neurotics demanding unnecessary operations, and he is forced to reopen his books on psychosomatic medicine. The sexually bold, religiously shy neurotic is often surgically courageous in a misguided effort to gain attention, meaning, and significance for his life.

Adler has taught us the important part played in life by the sense of inadequacy or inferiority. Developmental psychology has been fruitful in providing most helpful insights, but its popular treatment in periodical literature has given far too many parents unnecessary guilt feelings. They come to the conclusion that all personality failures are directly due to unwise handling of the child in the family, overlooking that there are other significant, contributory causes. Nevertheless there are parents who never wean their children psychologically, and they never wean themselves from an authoritarian role. They treat their children of all ages as though they always are the best babies in the world, shielding them in every possible way. Some school systems also contribute by grading methods that ignore individual differences, thus failing to handle adequately the needs of both the limited child and the gifted child. A student can play his way through high school and easily acquire a college degree by the simple expedient of " passing " required courses for the accumulation of " units " — only to be flunked out by life in the first, and second, and third jobs. Existential living presents the task of honestly facing limitations as well as capacities. But for the shielded individual this comes as a shock, and so he uses the Adlerian vocabulary as a semantic shield or philosophy, and excuses his refusal to face responsibility as an adult because of his complexes. He learns the vocabulary of defeat before he develops and flexes his spiritual muscles in the conflicts of life. Every counselor has abundant evidence in his work to illustrate these facts.

3. Logotherapy in Counseling

If it is true that cultural influences have contributed to the malaise of our time, this becomes a challenge for counseling as a form of therapy to utilize the insights of existential analysis in its treatment. As was indicated previously, the reader should not expect to find here a manual of technique. Many excellent books are available that deal with the techniques of counseling and psychotherapy. Existential analysis has its technical procedures, but these, as with other schools of psychotherapy, are tentative measures, to be adapted to situations and persons who are always treated as unique. Its particular contributions can be applied within the frame of reference of almost any psychotherapeutic orientation if the therapist is genuinely concerned with human suffering. Existential analysis as logotherapy does not pretend to be a finished procedure, for systems have a way of manipulating man to fit their theoretical presuppositions. It is developing and growing, and it invites co-operation and constructive criticism from those interested in sharing therapeutic insights. In Vienna existential logotherapy is carried out in individual and in group therapy, in clinical work and in clinical class demonstrations treating neurological and psychiatric patients. Similarities in other approaches are freely recognized, for the founder of logotherapy has pointed out in his writings the implications for logotherapeutic work in the teachings of Freud, Adler, Jung, and others.

For Frankl it is essential that there exist many methods of therapy, and this position is connected with his concept of man. " Psychotherapy," he says, " is an equation of X plus Y, wherein X stands for the individuality of the patient, differing from every other patient, and Y stands for the individuality of the doctor. To be most correct, we should invent a new therapy for each patient. Thus it follows that the therapeutic method chosen depends both upon X and Y, the choice being influenced by the individuality of both doctor and patient." [13] He points out that not every patient will respond to a particular method. Hypnotism, for example, has a place in the Vienna clinic, but it is definitely not used by every doctor, and of course not on every patient. This concern for the individuality of the patient stems from the logotherapeutic view of every man as a being who, in Frankl's words, " is unique in his essence, and singular in his existence." Though couched in medical language, the applicability of these principles to counselor and client is obvious.

The cause-and-effect relation of values in cultural creativity and in cultural decline, recognizable in Professor Sorokin's research, is matched by the relation of values to mental health stressed in logotherapy. The concept of man in logotherapy gives central importance to his particularly human qualities which include freedom, responsibility, meaning, and spirituality. The values man chooses and lives by either enhance these specifically human qualities or they tear them down, and the result is his existential frustration. The concepts of man that deny these specifically human attributes — Frankl calls them homunculisms — view man as a mere collection of driving forces, or a product of heredity plus environment, a complex of sense data, or as Bertrand Russell describes him, " a collection of molecules of protoplasm." These views vary as to whether a material mechanism or a biological organism serves as the prototype of man. The ancient view of man as made in the image of God was changed in the heyday of sensate culture to the view that conceived of him as a machine. Today in the age of electronic computors man becomes the "thinking machine," but to existential logotherapy all this is an aberration of what is specifically human.

The counselor interested in logotherapy will be stimulated by its concept of man and its interest in maintaining the dignity of man by re-examining the problem of meaning. In dealing with this in counseling, the relevance of meaning not only to the present and future is obvious, but its significance for the past also has value for therapy. In helping a client, depressed by the apparent meaninglessness of his life or of all life, the counselor can, of course, help him work through his feelings and difficulties in terms of the present meaninglessness and a possible significance for the future that may be arrived at. In so doing, Frankl has found that the existence of meaning in past experience can be utilized in therapy, for to realize this existence is "to rescue the past and what is stored in the past." For example, if a lonely person, feeling unloved and unwanted, is led to recall that he has experienced love – if only once – no additional unhappy experiences can obviate this fact or annihilate it. Whatever is in the past of meaningful experience and existence is, as Frankl teaches, not lost but forever thus saved from transitoriness. This emphasis Frankl has found also peculiarly helpful in dealing with potential suicidal clients as well as with those hospitalized as a result of suicide attempts. In this connection, Sorokin has compiled charts to show that in any culture when the relativization of values occurs or increases, the incidence of suicide also rises. Frankl summarizes this approach to the problem of meaning with a quotation from Lao-tze: "To have fulfilled a task means to have become eternal."

For many people the experience of unavoidable suffering and the fact of death seem to cancel out much, if not all, of their life's meaning. Along with all doctors, Frankl has faced this dilemma. He feels that therapy has a special function here rather than merely the giving of a gracious nod toward religion, and he has written a book on the problem of suffering.[14] His unusual authority for discussing the status of suffering man is based, not on theoretical presuppositions, but as we have seen, on the grueling experiences he underwent at the hands of nazi guards in concentration camps. To bodily punishments, illness, starvation, and the immanence of death were added the professional frustrations of a doctor trying to minister to patients suffering from virulent disease, with only a few aspirin tablets at his disposal, and this after serving a day at the hard labor of road-making. More soul-searching yet than this were his efforts to function as a psychotherapist both at work and at night after "lights out" when men in despair struggled with agonizing questions as to the meaning of such uncalled-for inhumanity of man to man, the meaning of suffering, the meaning of existence — of God. On transfer and entry to a new camp an efficiency expert would size up the wretched prisoners and decide with a nod of his head who was still capable of further work, and who would go immediately to the gas chamber. A man rejoiced to find himself in a new work camp, but only until he learned that his friend had been sent to the camp with the big chimney! This sort of thing is played down in Frankl's dispassionate account of the camps,[15] but no one can read it and fail to pay respect to his therapeutic work that was so tested, and which eventuates in his existential analysis.

With existence stripped down to the barest of essentials, all normal values completely absent, the men in concentration camps found tremendous spiritual support in discovering the value of the attitudes with which they faced their suffering. This was far more profound than the Stoic resignation to fate. And it was deeper than being a useful secret for survival, for it was also effective in the lives of those who did not survive. The essence of the matter is the discovery that suffering itself can be made meaningful and that it along with death is a test that man as existential *being* can successfully "pass." Or it can be seen as a valley of shadows through which one passes triumphant, not only over fears and terrors of environmental dangers, but triumphant over the greatest fear of all, that of meaningless existence. Suffering must not be confused either with sickness or with physical pain, though these may be its causes. These after all, and resignation, or a stoical way of putting up with them, man shares with the animals. It is precisely in *how* one faces suffering to find even there a deep meaning, in spite of not knowing its *why*, that man rises to a uniquely human achievement and thus demonstrates his spiritual dimension.

The question of the *why* leads to what Frankl has called " supermeaning," which transcends the boundaries of man's existence. Supermeaning signifies that which is not capable of being grasped with our minds as an intellectual task. This, however, does not mean that existence becomes meaningless, but that it calls for a response with our whole being, emotionally, morally, living to the fullest extent of meaning of which we are capable. Ultimately the question of the why is one of theodicy, and here Frankl quotes Einstein: " Science cannot provide a man with ultimate answers to ultimate questions: this is up to man's faith." To Frankl, " faith is not a kind of thinking; it is this, plus something: We think with our brains, but believe with the wholeness of our being." [16] From here it is but a step to the definition of faith as commitment, trust, and loyalty. At this point, too, comes the transition to what has been mentioned as " medical ministry," and though Frankl asserts therapists should not presume to answer questions of theodicy, they can nevertheless co-operate with the clergy without confusing the boundaries of their respective functions. It is agreed that ultimate questions are answerable only on an existential basis, in terms of man's whole being. But I would urge further that in so far as the counselor gets into another person's existence, as Rogers has so incisively described the experience, the emergence of ultimate questions creates a tension that often must be honestly faced — at the moment — and not shunted to the clergy!

The counselor interested in implementing in his therapy the

insights of existential logotherapy on suffering will have, first of all, to face his own existence and his own attitudes toward its meaning. His own theoretical orientation will indicate whether he will proceed in a directive, nondirective, or chiefly supportive way. Great gains have been made through Rogers' approach, though there are times, where information may be helpful to certain clients, that more directive guidance is necessary. Certainly, a great deal of supportive counseling already is in effect in the acceptance and understanding of the counselor, together with his ability to communicate these adequately. Assuming the counselor has had little experience in deep suffering, it follows that the sufferer, as client, has an advantage here in knowledge and experience, as well as the opportunity to transcend his difficulty — and his therapist! One sees this in the group therapy of mental hospitals, where schizophrenic patients, on the road to recovery, use insights they have gained to help other patients, and thus advance their recovery seemingly faster than in formal therapy.

In describing his feelings concerning the normal medical approach to suffering, Frankl writes: "A doctor who is sensitive to the imponderables of a situation will always feel a kind of shame when attending a patient with an incurable disease, or a dying person. For the doctor himself is helpless, incapable of wresting this victim from death. But the patient has become a hero who is meeting his fate and holding his own by accepting it in tranquil suffering. That is, on a metaphysical plane; a true achievement — while the doctor in the physical world, in his physician's realm, has his hands tied, is a failure." [17] It should be added here that if the doctor, as a counselor, has been instrumental in helping the patient achieve this attitudinal meaning and victory, he cannot consider his work a failure. Frankl's point is that where medicine fails, medical ministry carries on and remains a responsibility for the therapist. The founder of logotherapy frankly admits that many doctors have always carried out his principles in their practice. His work has served to make explicit what every good doctor knows and does.

In view of the use of values and responsibility in leading the patient to an appreciation of the meaning of his individual life, Frankl's school, as has been noted above, is very careful to insist that the patient discover his own values and make his own responsible decisions. The logotherapist definitely does not impose his own values upon the patient. This insistence is ontologically and logically the outcome of its doctrine of man as a being in three dimensions — somatic, psychic, and noetic or spiritual. Man does not really enter the noetic dimension or use its capacities until he recognizes and uses his freedom, makes real choices that result in the exercise of responsibility. He decides for values and goals that deepen the meaning of his singular existence.

Although refraining, along with the best of the nondirective tradition, from imposing values, the logotherapist in existential analysis feels at liberty, however, to point out the wide range of values that are available. Often enough the latent values, talents, and capacities of the client, which have been smothered by his frustration, depression, or anxieties, are realistically faced or discovered in therapy, and through a supportive technique the therapist encourages the client to realize these more fully in his existence. What had hitherto been an unknown, strange frontierland of value is explored together by client and therapist. This kind of value-therapy might be likened to the chemical laboratory where a catalyst is added to another substance with the effect of changing that substance into a different form without being incorporated into it or changing itself. The logotherapeutic doctor of souls is a catalytic agent who is useful, let us say, in precipitating values in the life of the patient, without projecting his own value system into the patient. He must accomplish this in order to be true to Frankl's existential concept of man as a free, responsible being with a will toward meaning who actualizes that meaning or the process of becoming by responsible choices that ultimately include attitudinal values. Any therapy that turns out dependent personalities, couch-happy clients who so enjoy the counseling relationship that they refuse to leave it, is not existential analysis, though it may have started as such. This is true, of course, of all therapies that aim at producing mature personalities: the therapist helps the client to find the way that must be traveled, but the client must decide himself to travel; he must choose the direction on the way (values, sensate or idealistic!) and he must walk alone, by his own strength. Anything short of this leaves the way lined with forlorn, neurotic hitchhikers, thumbing a ride from life, for they know how to travel only pickaback.

4. The Significance of Vocation

Vocational counseling, rather than a prosaic, routine activity embellished a bit with vocational interest and aptitude tests, can become an exciting adventure of seeing a reorganized personality start a new career of his own choosing. All specialists in vocational work have had the experience of watching a client change from a dull, apathetic, frustrated individual to one happily engaged in work that utilizes more of his real interests and capacities and that offers goals worth realizing. The existential approach can offer valuable help here with its insights into man's essential nature as a being who himself decides what he is becoming in the next moment. In vocational therapy the casebooks are full of stories of those who are frustrated in their daily jobs, often enough because they entered them under pressure. In other cases awareness is buried under strong conflicts. One patient at the Vienna polyclinic came from another country and asked to have his analysis continued as his former analyst had told him he was still tied to his father image. Fortunately — or unfortunately — he had had the means to pay for five years of analysis, but still was surfeited with father-image ideas. He was in Government work, but hated his job because it reminded him of his father who had forced it on him. The actual details of his work he did not hate at all. From the frame of reference of logotherapy it appeared that the analyst had treated him, not as a human being, but as a monad, an isolated item not in contact with the real world, for his father images were not real. The real challenge of making his own choice, assuming responsibility for the unique use of his own abilities and therefore deciding his own vocation had never been faced by this man. His basic problem was not a deep unconscious conflict but primarily vocational and existential, for it involved his own concept of himself. Short-term therapy enabled him to make his own vocational choice, which put new meaning into his life and turned him into a happy man at last able to make friends with his father.

The concept of responsibility in existential analysis means that man is responsible *for* the actualization of values in his life, and responsible *to* others, conscience, family, society, or God. Self-realization, important goal as it is in psychology, must still be related to a larger purpose or function: vocation and responsibility. For, in logotherapy, man is seen as not responsible for self-fulfillment or self-actualization primarily, but for the fulfillment of his own unique life's task. Then self-realization follows as a side effect. For many people daily work is not necessarily their life task, for no matter how significant or insignificant the work, what is more important is the manner in which it is done.

Sometimes people use their work status as an excuse or neurotic escape from the problem of self-realization as related to other values. They feel some other line of work would have better enabled them to be creative. Of this complaint Frankl writes: " If there are cases where the actual occupation does not allow a sense of fulfillment to arise, the fault is in the person, not in the work. The work in itself does not make the person indispensable and irreplaceable; it only gives him the chance to be so. It does not lie with the occupation, but always with us, whether those elements of the personal and the specific which constitute the uniqueness of our existence are expressed in the work and thus make life meaningful." [18] Everyone has within his acquaintance those people who are examples of the two laborers in the well-known anecdote: Asked what they were doing, one replied, " Chipping stones," and the other, " Building a cathedral." It is the different attitude that makes all the difference in the satisfactions and purposes a man finds in his work.

The change of words above from " vocation " to " work " was deliberately made. Everyone works, but not everyone's work is identical with his vocation. The person who is completely happy in his work sometimes has the two together. But the vocational counselor has to deal with many who are simply misfits in their jobs, who *have* missed opportunities, whose obvious talents were wasted or never developed. These present poignant problems at times when, at an age far beyond any reasonable hope of attaining their goal, they dream of or plan an extensive, radical change of job or profession. Here the existential emphasis does not follow the empty " develop a new hobby " approach, but calls attention to vocation, the fulfillment of a life's task, which can be achieved perhaps even in uncongenial employment, or again apart from it. This sort of thing occurs as individuals sometimes stumble upon it, and they find real happiness in doing what Frankl calls fulfilling a concrete personal task, a " mission " which may or may not be a result of conscious awareness of the unique meaning of singular existence.

Counseling can make use of the basically philosophical insights of existential analysis in therapy with clients who are vocationally unhappy. The retired person is either filled with ennui or he sometimes demonstrates creative bursts of energy. An example of our acquaintance is that of a man who had spent a long life in small businesses that eventuated at retirement in the most modest of economic security. In his seventies he became concerned over the appalling loneliness of the many people of his generation and gathered a few together in a " senior citizens club." In an extraordinarily short time he galvanized the entire community by his enthusiasm for his cause. Laborers, doctors, teachers, business men, and judges served on his committee and worked on a clubhouse for his senior citizens. The

" fulfillment of his life's task," which now serves as a pilot-plant for other interested communities, came completely apart from his preceding work, unless indeed that made him sensitively aware of the boredom that so many find in their daily work. Frankl likes to speak of values " calling " a man, in contrast to the teaching of other schools that stress the impulses that " drive " a man. After all, the word vocation comes from the Latin *vocare*, " to call," and to counsel a man to the achievement of his real calling, whether in his daily work or apart from it is a fine thing. It even, in the two-way satisfaction it engenders, helps the counselor in his own self-realization!

Developmental psychology has given profound insight into many personality problems with its portrayal of the tremendous significance of early influences, training, and conditioning. Trauma arising in this period can be long-lasting in deleterious effects, and in some cases irremediable. But we must not allow a myth of developmental determinism to arise from these facts — a pessimistic conclusion that, as has been remarked, allows some adults to use the Adlerian vocabulary as a semantic escape from responsibility. Personality development is far more like a living plant than the block of stone with which a sculptor starts. If his chisel or mallet slips as he is finishing a head and inadvertently cuts off the nose or an ear, the trauma is truly irremediable. He must start with a new stone. The growing tree that has been topped will send up a new branch, which now becomes the new growing point, and personality can do the same thing. This truth is evidenced both in family life and in the adult education movement. A parent can make grievous mistakes with a child. But a parent also can realize this and even become " big " enough to learn how to apologize, in words and actions, to his own child. And a child can forgive, much more easily than an adult. Even in a given situation where the unhappily ingrained authoritarian attitudes of the parents create rebelliousness in children who react by rejecting as adults the values of the parents, all is not lost. Allport states in this connection that where the attitudes and motives of the parents are well meant, though their implementation was poor, the children tend to return to the values of the parents, but without the authoritarian elements, when they reach maturity.[19]

A great many vocational and marriage difficulties can be traced easily to their source in family influences, but the counselor gets little help from dwelling too long on causes, particularly if his concern is for the client to accept responsibility for choosing his own values, and choosing them not merely in reaction to his parents' values. Pertinent here is the wisdom of Aristotle: "Better is the end of a thing than the beginning thereof."

Adult education presents a more formal refutation of developmental determinism. Though of course the early years when the child is most malleable remain the most important, it does not follow that they are the only important years for development. Sheldon long ago pointed out that certain disciplines, such as philosophy, are grasped better in maturity than in the callow college years.[20] The tremendous contributions in the arts and sciences by people who come late to the realization of their creativity also gives the counselor additional proof of man's ability to utilize freedom for choosing responsibility in the face of many determining limitations. Certainly the dull life of a Parisian bank clerk gave little indication of the artistic genius lurking in a Gauguin. Psychoanalysis itself is based upon the premise that people can change, and it does change them if its time requirements for therapy can be met. The apathetic adage "You can't teach an old dog new tricks" used as an escape from facing the vocational challenge was long ago refuted by adult education. To change from the figurative to the real animal world, it is also refuted by zoo keepers, who report that their animals that are given "work" to do live longer than those maintained in idleness. There are values and purpose in all existence, even in zoo existence! Adult education is a better illustration. In one small but well-organized college with an enrollment of one thousand regular students, an adult program enrolls approximately eight thousand adults in evening classes in the sciences, humanities, and arts. The adult with a flexible mind can keep that mind alert and even stave off senility by the development of his potentials as long as he lives.

The growth of technology and automation has given large segments of the population more leisure time than has ever been known in most civilizations and cultures. If a man's work, vocation, values, and the meaning of his existence are not fairly intimately related, the result is what Frankl has called existential vacuum. If work, even though creative and with many satisfactions, becomes an end in itself, or is used as an escape from more important responsibilities and values, the poverty of existence soon becomes evident. No therapist or counselor wants to play God or operate as a tinker of souls, even though the neurotic places him *in loco Dei* with his demand: "Here is my problem; now tell me what to do." Even divine omniscience does not accede to direct demands, and no theoretical orientation has yet claimed omniscience, despite Bertrand Russell's well-known tease: "Every man would like to be God if it were possible; some few find it difficult to admit the impossibility." [21] Theology would remind us that values are of the things of God, and the counselor, aware of the direct and subtle influence of values on culture and personality, will be sensitive to his responsibility of meeting his share of the critical difficulties of our era when they revolve about value and meaning.

The work of the counselor often covers the same range as that of all psychotherapy except that dealing with the psychoses and the deeper neuroses. Existential analysis is relevant to counseling in areas such as those of the disturbed child, adolescence, sex problems, delinquency, marriage, family relations, and other fields. One brief reference to love and marriage counseling may be apropos here. In *The Doctor and the Soul,* Dr. Frankl devotes fifty pages to the meaning of love in which he explores sex, love, marriage, and some youth problems as well. Scheler defines love as a movement of the mind toward the highest possible value of the loved person, a spiritual act in which this highest value — which he calls the "salvation" of a person — is apprehended.[22] This highest possible value, as a potentiality in essential reality is not a matter of calculation, least of all in psychotherapy, which, as Frankl teaches, should "combine the spirit of love with the kindness of the teacher." Again, "It is part of the metaphysical mystery of the spiritual act we call love that out of the beloved's essential image it succeeds in reading the valuational image."

Frankl here reminds one of Shakespeare's "Love is not love which alters when it alteration finds," for the mature lover helps the beloved to become or actualize the personal values seen by the eyes of love. Each in turn seeks to become a more worthy recipient of love, by growing more into the likeness of the lover's image. He denies the existence of unrequited love, holding that if genuine love was present, even though unreturned, the lover nevertheless is enriched. (Does not Dante in his love for Beatrice also have something to say that verifies this?) Therefore, "even 'unrequited love' enriches us and brings happiness, while 'requited' love is distinctly creative. In mutual love, in which each wishes to be worthy of the other, to become like the other's vision of him, a kind of dialectical process takes place in which each outbids the other and so elevates the other." [23]

This may appear to some people to be an impossibly idealistic version of love in view of the tough problems arising from the unrealistic expectations of those who find wedded bliss no solution to their personality difficulties. Others, stimulated by the interest of psychiatry in the powerful dynamic of love will carry on from there. To Frankl, real love has the requirement of being erotically mature enough for a monogamous relationship. He identifies three steps, levels, or stages of development: sex attraction, which brings pleasure, erotic infatuation, which brings joy, and the love relationship, which brings happiness. His exposition of this area of his thought has brought some sharp criticism from writers who were limited to his earlier, briefer writings, but they nevertheless honor his logotherapy with extended discussion and evaluation.[24]

A word on communication is added here, for it is an item so obvious that it can easily be assumed without being actualized. This is because of its relation to the personal needs, limitations, and values of the counselor. Theory can hinder communication if it moves in too early to pounce upon the attempted communication of the client in order to categorize his revelations, conflicts, feelings, or self-concept. Existential logotherapy would remind us to be responsive to the whole man, not to his id impulses at this moment and to the difference between superego controls and ego involvement at the next moment. It has long been a platitude that counseling should be person-centered, not problem-centered. A person who is attempting to communicate his deep feelings in therapy should be accepted as he is at the present moment of his existence, and his feelings deserve to be treated as fact, however divorced from reality they may seem to theory. Even though valuable insights may be gained from apparent indication of id elements, let us say, these remain secondary to the existential here-and-now relationship of client and counselor, patient and psychiatrist.

The therapist also needs to communicate to the client the fact that he accepts and understands. His communication can be effective even when nonverbal or quasi-verbal. A good nondirective response may be an excellent *intellectual* clarification, but an apathetic, monotonous tone of voice may fail to communicate. Methodology may defeat communication as in the case of the therapist who habitually seats his client and then courteously but determinedly waits for the client to begin speaking. One patient, being forewarned of this technique, resolved to make the doctor speak first. " After waiting exactly twenty minutes in silence," she reported, " my sense of humor got the best of me. I laughed and started talking." Here it follows that valuable therapy time might have been saved by a slight adjustment by the therapist, but on the other hand, the humor engendered may have been a therapeutic factor! The technique, attitudes, intention of the counselor, may be ideal, but communication can still be defeated by the anxiety of the counselor, however subtle its indicator. The sensitive client can catch the slightest of nuances here! Certain attitudes, mannerisms, clock-watching, the hypnotic gaze at the patient, or the faraway gaze *through* him or at the window — these not only distract him but often snap the slender thread of communication from counselor to client.

5. Group Therapy

Group therapy, which originated in Europe and went into a temporary decline during the period of nazi domination, is carried on in the Vienna clinic, along with individual therapy. The accents of existential logotherapy that have been examined in this book are those on singularity, or uniqueness, and individuality as these relate to freedom, choice, and responsibility. This results in an individual therapy that is more or less tailored to fit the needs of each patient, for after basic principles have been laid down, the healing process, as in any school of therapy, depends upon how therapist and patient incorporate or " incarnate " these principles in the relationship they accomplish together. Now there are other accents in the Vienna school that lend themselves well to group work. These are the wholeness and unity of man, aspects of responsibility toward others, his transcendence of self and self-concerns, his noetic dimension in which he is " pulled " by transcendent values that have little meaning except as they are related to the community. Dr. Ackerman, professor of psychiatry at Columbia University, writes in a recent journal: " Psychoanalysis has no real cure to offer for the agonizing loneliness and boredom of modern man. By tradition, individual psychotherapy, especially psychoanalysis, focuses on the internal economy of the personality. . . . [It] is a therapy which points selectively to past distortions in child-parent relations. It does not afford access ordinarily to the whole person in action in the community here and now." [25] The fact is, mental health or maturity, is not a static, finished state in anyone. It depends upon the capacity to handle and relate to new situations and ongoing processes, just as a healthy body maintains a capacity to resist infection in its relation to the environment. In mental health the individual remains open and alert to new experience, which enables him to grow not only in self-appreciation but also in the understanding of others.

The chief function of group therapy is to provide an experimental community, a sort of laboratory experiment in human relations, where through psychodrama or role-playing group members practice the art and ways of relating to one another. Dramatic ability occasionally exhibited in role-playing can often enough stimulate discussions by the group, but the chief impetus for earnest group involvement is provided when difficulties and failures in interpersonal relations are discussed. I shall never forget one meeting of the Vienna group of which I was a member. Dr. Kocourek, the group leader, had assigned an elderly woman to play a relatively innocuous role. On taking her chair, she asked the doctor if she could choose a different role. He agreed and then she announced to the group: " I shall play the role of my own life. I am old and tired and all alone. My only son has just died and I have no other relatives. Since my income is so low, I lost my apartment, my only home. I tried to commit suicide, and that's why I am here, for I see utterly no sense in living this kind of a life, no meaning at all." The man assigned to play the role opposite her was visibly startled, but he had had considerable group experience and started in rapid speech to comfort her. Her personal tragedy, however, so aroused the sympathy and anxieties of the group that role-playing was abandoned in a few moments, and almost two hours of intense discussion ensued in which the shyest members, who hitherto had never spoken voluntarily, took part. Some of the anxiety of the group members was due to the fact that several of them were also suicidal patients. The sudden and candid expression of a difficulty common to several members of the group sparked the agitated discussion, with the resultant release of a lot of emotion. The conclusion that life could be meaningful under any and all circumstances was arrived at by the group.

Psychotherapists became interested in group work not only because of its economy of time but also because it is a more effective way of meeting some difficulties. Its very structure provides built-in safeguards or solutions for such well-discussed problems as transference, hostility, and authoritarian roles, for these tend to be diffused throughout the group and not focused upon a therapist. The group leader is really more of a convener than a leader and never dominates the group: the success of the interplay of group dynamics depends to a significant extent on the way the leader submerges himself as a therapist and participates fully as a member.

In advocating that the doctor also consider himself a patient in group activity Dr. Ackerman writes: "I have myself purposely experimented with this aspect of the problem by opening myself wide in the group and have been gratified to find that the experience was therapeutic for me as well as for the patients." [26] In my own experience with group therapy I have noted that it is easier for psychologically oriented therapists to effect this identification with the group than for those who are medically oriented. This is not due to any superiority of psychology, as a few have covertly assumed, but is a result of the fact that our society casts the medical man in a prestige and authoritarian role, from which he has to extricate himself before a group accepts him as a participating member. The doctor's problem here is similar to that of the clergyman whom society usually tries to put on a pedestal to serve as its official superego.

The clergyman almost invariably is cast into an authoritarian role by the expectations of his parishioners, and this fact must be dealt with if he is to function adequately. The Christian church, which began as a small group movement, has never entirely lost sight of the group approach. Though the accent was not usually upon the therapeutic value, this occasionally was realized in group relationships. Renewed interest in the significance of group work now matches the attention given to pastoral counseling, and it is to this responsibility of the clergyman that we turn in the final chapter of this discussion of the frontier area between psychotherapy and religion.

Chapter V

Logotherapy and Pastoral Psychology

1. Pastoral Psychology in Relation to Psychotherapy

The pastor, regardless of whether he has been trained in psychotherapy or counseling, cannot escape the responsibilities of working in the field of pastoral psychology. Even should he want to escape, his people will not let him. If he resists their interests and needs here, he finds himself isolated and insulated, preaching an ethic that does not get through to ethos. This does not mean, either, that the total emphasis of the pastor is just on psychological needs. His people have other needs of which they often are not aware, and his spiritual ministry includes the responsibility of bringing these needs to consciousness. The pastor's own interests, resulting from his vocation, training, and dedication to the prophetic phase of God's work, must be carried to congregation and community through education, preaching, prayer, worship, fellowship, and pastoral visiting of the healthy as well as the sick. The concern of the ancient and medieval church with healing has returned today in the concern of the modern pastor with counseling and its implications for healing. In all this, the wrong turn can make of the pastor merely an errand boy for an overgrown and ingrown institution, and its public relations expert to the community. The right turn can get him so deeply involved in trying to meet expectations and demands upon his time that physical breakdown is not an unusual occurrence.

The term " pastoral psychology " suggests wider areas of the

144

clergyman's work than just the counseling ministry, in which historically rabbi, priest, and minister have always been involved. The name is more accurate than the expression "pastoral psychiatry," which is a misleading contradiction.[1] Psychiatry is a medical discipline, carried on only by a medically trained doctor who has a legal license to practice medicine. The pastor too is licensed, but by his church, and that license is recognized by law only to the extent that most state law requires pastors who perform marriages to be so recognized by their church. Whether this protects the minister from legal complications resulting from counseling is a matter yet to be tested in the courts. In the very few cases where a psychiatrist is also an ordained clergyman, he does not function as a pastor when he practices psychiatry. If he carries on pastoral work, all the advantages of psychiatric training and experience are at his disposal, of course, just as theological insight may make him a better psychiatrist. He is like the concert master of the symphony who may also be a good teacher, but who, at the concert, is not an instructor but a violinist.

The minister, therefore, does not function as a psychiatrist, nor as a psychologist, even though he may possess a doctor's degree in psychology. Counseling, vitally important as it is, also remains subsidiary to the fact that the pastor is a specialist in his own right, so recognized and set apart by his church. His speciality is that of minister of the Word of God, and as the phrase indicates, the word "minister" is out of context unless it be understood in relationship to the Word of God. The *Logos* (Word) of Greek philosophy, vitalized in John's Gospel, appropriated by Frankl to revitalize psychotherapy, means to the prophetic ministry of the church precisely the word that God addresses to men to show them the way of life. The chief responsibility of the pastor, then, is to show in every possible way the relevance of the Word of God (revealed, written, and living) to the birth, life, and death of every living soul.

The word "prophetic," as I use it here, is not intended to

carry any connotations of divine soothsaying or the prediction of future events. This is but a minor element in the phenomena, and vastly overemphasized by certain religious cults that continually strive to put divine and eternal events that are beyond time into human time schedules figured with the mathematical precision of a railroad timetable. Biblical scholarship has made it clear that the prophets of Judaism conceived of their prime function as that of mouthpieces speaking for the holy, invisible One, who had so impressed the reality of his existence and requirements upon their being that they could not remain silent in the face of human need, cruelty, and injustice! They were "existentialists" long before that term became current in modern usage. The history of religions in turn has to deal with this as a unique phenomenon. All religions, of course, have had prophets of a sort. But prophets who spoke, convinced that they were speaking for the *one* high and holy Creator and Lord of the universe, are confined to the Judaeo-Christian tradition.

The pastor carries on in the tradition of the prophets with the conviction that what God accomplished in the lives of men in the past always awaits accomplishment in the lives of men of today. The Word of God is not confined to the past, nor to the pages of the Bible where some earnest souls would imprison it today. Thus the pastor, while doing important work in pastoral psychology and being grateful for insights from psychotherapy, should carry on in full awareness of other and deeper sources of power that he is to help release in his people. His unique vocation and function stem primarily neither from the authority of a Bible or a church but from his intuitive awareness (just as in the case of the prophets) that God communicates with man in living relationships. This experience of man with God is the ultimate test and ground for the authority of the church and the Bible. The Scriptures of the Bible serve to describe the relationships of men and nations, as well as the evasions and failures to find satisfaction and fullness of life in other ways of living. The historic facts as stressed in Christianity, together with the Scriptures as related to man's experience with God and God's word to man, are the ground for the existence of the church. This highly condensed account of some important background elements of pastoral work, in addition to the following description of theological training, is included here chiefly to orient the non-theologically trained reader, and in the interests of furthering the understanding and relationships of religion and psychotherapy.

The particular training, skills, and methodology of the psychotherapist need not be reviewed here, but a statement of the training and special skills of the pastor might be helpful. He is trained in a professional school, called a Theological Seminary, or a School of Religion, for a period of three to four years, after first completing four years of college or university. His professional training includes theology and philosophy, history, Biblical research and languages, ethics, education, psychology, preaching, music, church administration, missions, group work and drama, techniques of audio-visual education, and a field-work program that partially corresponds to the interne program of the doctor of medicine. Other subjects taught are familiar enough to the pastor, but the subjects listed suffice to acquaint others with the general education of pastors. Very few Protestant theological schools have preparatory educational requirements such as those expected by the schools of law or medicine. Most educators feel that this should be the case, and the professional training itself should be extended to four years. A full year of interne pastoral work under supervision is now required by a few denominations.

To the formal training of the pastor is added the expectation that he should develop mature experience in, and profound appreciation of, the less tangible but the most significant elements of his religion which have been tested over the centuries by all forms of mature religion. These include faith, hope, and love, so familiar as almost to have become platitudes in the thought of man. Emil Brunner has rescued them from platitudinous expression by demonstrating in his book of the same name their profound implications for medical and pastoral psychology. Faith relates man correctly to the past, with its burden of sin, guilt, and failure that crowds so unhappily into the present, by releasing God's forgiveness in his life, God's *acceptance* of him despite his sin. Hope relates man correctly to the future, with its forboding anxieties and uncertainties, by affirming God's ultimate rule and that, therefore, " God has a stake in history! " With the past no longer crowding the present with guilt, and the future no longer rushing in with anxiety, the present (all but squeezed out of existence by pressures of past guilt and future anxiety) no longer need be barren of love. Properly related to time — past, present, and future — man now is free to learn the richness and full meaning of love. Thus Paul's classic expression of the lyric poetry of religious experience is seen to have not only religious but also therapeutic significance.

Faith has been discussed in terms of loyalty and commitment, and contrasted with the mistaken idea of agreement to a required number of propositions. The pastor personalizes faith as commitment to the person of Jesus Christ, who in turn is recognized as God's self-revelation to humanity. Hope speaks to the anxious world of today by reminding the pastor to remind his people that the fearful forces loosed in our modern world are still under the judgment of God who alone is omnipotent. No further qualifications on love need be added in this context of psychotherapy and religion. So excellent are the descriptions of mature love to be met with in psychiatric literature today that they sound like a movingly earnest echo of the teaching of the Carpenter from Nazareth. Others of the less tangible elements of the pastor's experience include prayer and worship. Prayer is not a magical manipulation and bargaining with Deity but communion and relationship, graciously invited by an inexpressibly holy Being, who seeks the expression of his will in man's daily living. Worship is not the emotional catharsis sometimes seen in cults, but it is praise, awe, and prayerful reverence for the transcendent God who still concerns himself with our life and affairs. These are some of the "means of grace" in the pastor's spiritual arsenal, at his disposal in meeting the needs, conflicts, and tragedies of his people as well as their joys and expectations. When they are neglected or misused, human suffering is intensified just as it is in wrong treatment or diagnosis in psychotherapy.

The church today is aware that disabling mental illness can result from threatening situations, unwholesome environment, inadequate and hostile relationships, for this is a religious as well as a medical fact. Thus the training of the pastor turns, in all departments of a theological school, to the actualizing of what Jesus called the abundant life in all departments of human life. The church, without relinquishing faith in the transcendent "other world," sees itself responsible for implementing God's purpose and activity for the expression and fulfillment of life as far as possible here and now. This means helping people to prepare for life — for marriage, parenthood, family, group, and community living, together with the responsibilities inherent in these relationships. The church meets the problem of suffering with the ministry of consolation, but its tremendous affirmation that life is stronger than death, which is caught up in the extraordinarily profound doctrine of resurrection, has not adequately been mediated to modern man. Medieval piety was surfeited with references to death, and in our modern reaction to morbidity we avoid, even in Christian churches, mention of the word "death" itself, with euphemistic terminology appropriate enough for a lodge funeral but not for the Christian fellowship. In logotherapy, the insistence on the meaning of life that is not cancelable by death, values realizable in suffering, and the dignity of death, can help the pastoral ministry of consolation regain a balance here.

Emphasis upon what psychotherapy and religion have to offer each other is unnecessary in view of the fact that each has borrowed from the other. How this came about is described by Gordon Allport: " For the most part, psychotherapists employ implements borrowed from the clergy. The reason is simple enough: until recent times, the church alone dealt with problems of personality. The borrowed devices include listening, encouragement, advice, and the relationship of transference wherein the applicant finds security in dependence upon his counselor." [2] The time has come for psychotherapy and religion to recognize boundaries, to address themselves to the task of clarifying the frontierland of personality in which both are active in healing the hurt of man. An earlier chapter urged the church to broaden its concept of man to include certain aspects of the psychiatric knowledge of man. The contributions of Allport, Roberts, Sherrill, Frankl, and others have pointed out directions here. The activity at both ecumenical and denominational levels of the church suggest that it is approaching this task.[3] It is also reasonable to ask psychotherapy to deepen its concept of man, and to take a longer look at God! For the existential analysis of Frankl and the cultural analysis of Sorokin both discover that man gets frustrated, neurotic, and sick when his transcendental capacities, which point to a realization beyond his natural existence, are thwarted, when he finds no meaning in his life, when his values are completely sensate.

Experienced pastors willingly admit that Freud's stricture on religion has a certain validity. It is true not only that some neurotics but many others are arrested at the level of childhood imagery as far as religious growth is concerned. Such simple souls in their form of piety project God as a celestial Santa Claus, " the man upstairs," or as a member of the jukebox generation called him, " a livin' doll." Of course, such fantasies of God exist, they have always existed, and today this fantastic God is worshiped in jukebox gospel songs in livin' rhythm! One man sought to avoid the anthropomorphism that is inescapable in life and religion, and reported that he no longer conceived of God as a bearded man, but as " a vague, oblong blur." The concept of God as energy is no less anthropomorphic than that of God as Father, for we learn about energy from our human use of force or energy to overcome resistance.

All this type of imagery is far removed from the utterly holy God of the austere monotheistic prophets who dared speak out in the midst of a polytheistic culture where decadence was deified. It is not the God that Jesus described as the heartbroken father of the prodigal son, nor yet the Wholly Other of Barth and the eternal Thou of Buber. Freud's dogma raises the questions of why and how these latter "projected" God as they did, leaving the Christian doctrines of inspiration and revelation out of consideration. We also are left with the question why *any* man projects God in the way Freud has described. For, if a man's earthly father is adequate and kindly, why does he need a heavenly symbol? If the earthly parent is rejecting and inadequate, why project a father, or whence arise the ideas of a better, heavenly one? Perhaps Augustine has the answer to these questions with his whimsical: "O God, thou has put salt upon our tongues so that we are everlastingly thirsty for thee." Any argument with the details of the great constructive work of Freud must not be allowed to obscure the fact that he has done religion a real service, actually a prophetic service, in pointing out our evasions of the real God, the substitutions of our own making, and significantly, our *need* of the Transcendent, which is so deeply seated that if God does not exist, we are driven to "project" a god. What Freud describes as projection, and Augustine as thirst, the Bible teaches is man's creation in the image (personality potential) of his Creator. Thus the eternal thirst of man can never be assuaged by jukebox religion whose surface balm does not penetrate to man's deeper needs. Another authority on man's ills, Jesus, spoke of a living water for this thirst. If Tillich is right in asserting that there is awareness of the meaning of grace, and resultant effective care of souls in depth psychology, the pastor must see that psychiatry has begun to draw upon the living water, and he himself must be all the more aware of the futility of doling out Coca-Cola religion to the congregation.

To return for a moment to the educational program of theological schools, we shall see that one of its goals is a clarification of the common interests of medical and pastoral psychology. In my classes each year one of the guest lecturers is a psychoanalyst who is agnostic and naturalistic in his outlook. He does not have to "relate analysis to religion" or force pious conclusions into the Freudian framework. He is perfectly free to describe God as a projection, and usually does. The responsibility of a Christian frame of reference remains that of the students who always rise to this challenge with questions, discussion, and sometimes a recognition of this as an opportunity to examine and deepen their own convictions. The student gains a knowledge of how other disciplines operate and an appreciation of values inherent in a naturalistic approach to human problems. The guest analysts happen to fit Tillich's description of those who are aware of grace, and they exemplify this not only in therapy but in the generous giving of their time to community mental-hygiene projects. Other specialists in delinquency, clinical psychology, and alcoholism are called upon to contribute their insights to the training of theological students. Training programs in nearby mental and general hospitals and corrective institutions give the opportunity for clinical experience to test theory. This procedure is followed in all theological schools that are alert to the implications of medical psychology for pastoral work. Some medical schools, as well as the Menninger clinic, are bringing in theologians for a similar purpose of relating pastoral psychology to medical and psychiatric training.

In many areas throughout the country, psychotherapists and pastors are meeting regularly in seminar discussions and conferences to explore one another's minds, attitudes, and common interests. Anxiety and guilt, often just convenient catchalls of therapy, cannot help having their etiology and treatment better understood if the best of thinking in both pastoral and medical psychology is brought to bear upon them. Through the centuries, beginning with Jesus' own awareness of the destructive effects of anxiety upon personality, Christian thought has addressed itself to this problem, with one culmination in the discernment of Kierkegaard.[4] Guilt, like anxiety, exists in both neurotic and real forms. Psychological discussion sometimes gives the impression that guilt is an unfortunate way of thinking, or that it is a thing, an entity, or vestigial organ of the psyche, like the appendix that may become inflamed and need surgical excision. Religious treatment is sometimes content to rest with the assertion and description of man's sin without clarifying in detail how forgiveness is mediated.

At a recent seminar discussion a pastor suggested that guilt is tied to sin, which, translated from the Greek *hamartia,* means "missing the mark." This sparked the interest of psychiatrists present who previously had reacted against the stereotyped notion of sin as confused with transgressions or identified with violations of social mores. Three hours of debate followed concluding with the general agreement that the source of man's guilt often lies in his deep conviction of failure to measure up to a standard. Until matters like these are explored, psychiatrists and the clergy merely spin their wheels by borrowing ideology from each other, or by discussing guilt and anxiety in general. Psychiatry certainly aids the neurotic whose vague feelings of guilt have him washing his hands after every handshake. Logotherapy reminds us that guilt and responsibility keep company. Theology stresses the existential guilt that rises in man's sin of self-worship which leads inevitably to failures in the relationships of man to man and man to God. One outcome of mutual exploration here can be the avoidance of defensive and authoritarian attitudes, as well as the protection of the freedom of both psychotherapy and religion.

Psychotherapy, following the Socratic dictum, "Know thyself," has provided us with vivid pictures of man's alienation from himself and his fellow man. Pastoral psychology, following Paul's injunction to "know as we are known," sees man as alienated also from God, and until he comes to know God, he cannot truly know himself. The relationship of man and God is basic and influential in every other relationship of man's existence! Religion, therefore, is not therapy, and even in pastoral counseling the ultimate aim is not solving difficulties, curing emotional ills, or the growth of personality. The pastor shares these goals with every therapist. The plus in his work (while of course avoiding sermonizing in counseling) is to mediate the knowledge of God without which self-knowledge is incomplete, and lacking which the self never achieves selfhood. The infant has the experience of *other-self* before it comes to awareness of self: this is the beginning of relationships that ultimately include God. When the adult sees himself as called into existence by *Other-Self*, God, then he begins to appreciate the wholeness of being of which the self is capable. This self-appreciation may, in part at least, account for the tremendous bursts of creative energy one sees in the history of man's achievements in the arts, in religion, and in science.

Religion, although not a therapy, in its intuitions, revelations, and experiences has often functioned as a powerful therapeutic agent in individual healing and cultural influence. Psychotherapy, though it demonstrates religious power, is not a religion: even as therapy it does not clearly understand itself if divergence in theory means anything, nor has it properly appraised the man it heals. But it functions as a powerful, dramatic agent in personality reorganization, and enables many to return to religion with more maturity. It has borrowed important weapons from the spiritual arsenal of the clergy. It has used them with such telling effect that it is sometimes necessary to remind those of the clergy who get too enamored of such weapons that they had a spiritual origin!

The time has arrived, therefore, for the clergy, in full awareness of what religion has given to, as well as gained from, psychotherapy, to take stock of their own incalculable resources in a bold reappraisal of what religion has to offer despairing man, anxious, neurotic, and lost man. Even the evangelist's thunderings against man as "lost, doomed, and damned" can be salvaged for religion if we stay with the Biblical meaning of "lost" and do not add the lurid illumination of Dante's *Inferno* that has provided more imagery for both Catholic and Protestant religion than the Bible itself! In New Testament Christianity the oldest name for this religion was simply *the way*. Being lost meant just what it says — lost — those who had lost their way, strayed from the only way that could lead them to their ultimate destination. The lost individual is he who has found more interesting detours that have tempted him from the King's Highway. These, fascinating at first, always dwindle to a rutted track and then tend to disappear in the sands, the desert wasteland of the isolated self. Jesus' analogy for this was the story of the good shepherd who, on returning his flock to the corral, found one missing, lost, and so he went out to seek and find the lost member of the "community." This precisely is a function of the church as the redemptive community, to save the lost by making them "unlost," by guiding them back to the "way." The church in its social concern also needs to be continually patching the chuckholes in the King's Highway so that the detours do not everlastingly provide tempting competition!

The Biblical view of the lost and the descriptions of neurosis found in the detailed writings of the neo-orthodox school of analysis have so many things in common that one is led to suspect that they are describing the same condition of man. This does not require the clergy to extol analysis merely because it confirms the Biblical view of man, for the latter also is based upon a lot of human experience and spiritual research. The analogy of "the way," though based on a Biblical fact, may seem an oversimplification to those concerned with the tragic elements of man's existence as these are vividly portrayed both in theological discussion and in the crises of current history. It is not intended to suggest a return to the easy liberalism of the nineteenth century, which dismissed hell as an anachronistic survival of medieval ideas of punishment. What can be dispensed with is the sulphurous concept unhappily still persisting in some areas of the church. In all of Jesus' many references to hell we find a realistic description of the torment of man who is alienated from himself, from his fellow man, from his God. The torments of hell are the individual suffering and loneliness of the man who has warped, narrowed, denied, and otherwise failed to develop the infinite potentialities of his life, according to Jesus. He puts the matter succinctly: "For what is a man advantaged, if he gain the whole world, and lose himself" (Luke 9:25, KJV). The findings of psychoanalysis thus are but a confirmation of the New Testament concept of hell as the separation of man from God and his fellow man.

It is in the context of man's alienation that the clergy can also utilize the contributions of Frankl's logotherapy. Where psychoanalysis lays bare the diseased tissue of man's very soul, logotherapy finds the source of the disease in the frustration man feels when the meaning of his life is not realized. Logotherapy goes farther in suggesting ways in which meaning can be attained, in the face of what appear to be insurmountable odds, by its emphasis upon attitudinal values. The naturalist, comfortably distanced by his objectivity (and boasted lack of personal bias), may dismiss this sort of thing as one more flying buttress to support the decrepit structure of religion, but only if the clergy pounce upon it as such. Despite attacks of enemies, well-meant intentions of friends, and failures of believers, Christianity and God will survive the ages. More important to recognize is that, in existentialism, philosophy is ready to speak of man in terms of transcendence, a subject upon which religion should be expert, for in this frontierland its spiritual researchers have done considerable exploration. And when existential analysis in logotherapy is ready to speak of "leaving the door open" to transcendental values, suggesting a validity to what lies beyond as well as the limitations of therapy, religion must be ready to pass through that door to test validity, for this is its particular province. The day may yet come when psychology will be enabled to take down its defenses against the spiritual dimension of man that it erected in the days of its adolescent rebellion.

2. Pastoral Psychology as Preventive Medicine

An area where pastoral psychology can make use of logotherapy is in viewing counseling, pastoral visiting, church education, group work, and even the sermon as opportunities for practicing " preventive medicine." The unique opportunity of the pastor to influence family living, the fact that normally he is not only welcome in the homes of his parishioners but also in those of the community in general, gives him an advantage not usually available to psychotherapists. Dr. Weisskopf-Joelson holds that " for a minister to be psychologically trained is today of utmost importance. Because of the minister's strategic importance in the community, people will go to him for help who normally would never go to a psychiatrist with their troubles." This lays upon the clergy the responsibility of seeing sickness of all kinds not only in relation to health as a norm but with respect to the still unhappily prevalent misconception of disease as a judgment or visitation of God because of sin. This ancient distortion is rejected by enlightened believers because of the significance of the healing miracles of Christ. Even simple logic should tell us that if sickness is a punishment for sin, we all ought to be sick all the time! It does not follow that God is not concerned with sickness, for here the mystery of his transcendence and immanence is involved, and God works in and through sickness. The ancient error that sickness, disability, or death is a punishment for sin is decisively rejected by Jesus in his reference to the murder of some Galileans, the fall of the tower of Siloam, and the man born blind. Of the latter he said. " It was not that this man sinned, or his parents, but that the works of God might be made manifest in him " (John 9:3). The problem of evil, insoluble to philosophy, portrayed in the drama of Job, here has a sharp ray of light played upon it which nevertheless does not enlighten the whole matter. For here is a mystery in which God's love and providence, man's failure and potential, are inextricably intertwined from the human point of view. But Jesus' words and action leave us with a challenge: we cannot rest with philosophical discussions of evil until we have done everything we can to alleviate its effects and comfort its victims.

Full appreciation of the fact that physical as well as mental health is part of the abundant life taught by Jesus should not blind our eyes to the fact that sin complicates matters, even though it is not the cause of disease. Repentance, forgiveness, love, and wholeness are dynamics found in Jesus' healing methods in dealing with human need. The insight that tangled emotions can cause bodily ailments was known to Jesus long before it issued in our categories of psychogenic and psychosomatic. His untying of emotional tangles resulted in physical health. All this does not mean that the gospel guarantees physical health in this kind of world. That was the mistake made by Mary Baker Eddy, but her emphasis of the role played by mental attitudes on bodily states was not a mistake, if the idea is not pushed too far. After all, Mrs. Eddy had to die too. The relevance of health to the abundant life must be dealt with in Christianity, else the miracles present problems more serious than the question of how they were accomplished. The greater number of them had to do with healing, and Jesus always took pains to avoid the magical approach, refusing to perform as a proof or " sign." Occasionally a sudden somatic change that occurs during psychotherapy will remind people of the healing miracles, as will be seen in the following case. A patient who had been thoroughly examined by her physician was referred for consultation. The doctor knew that the symptoms of Mrs. X, though disturbingly similar to a serious heart ailment, were not physically caused. One problem was that she was able to sleep only fitfully, sitting upright in bed because of a pounding heart and feelings of suffocation that had her literally gasping for air. Various possible roots of the difficulty in attitudes and relationships were explored by the patient and counselor. The basic difficulty appeared twofold: a deep resentment at what she considered stinginess on the part of her husband, and then, a failure of communication — her inability or fear of discussing this and other intimate matters with him. Counseling brought out the fact that the husband's concern for family security had led him to invest heavily in insurance on his life. He had further undertaken the purchase of a home and was paying off the mortgage with such large monthly payments that too little was left over in his budget for household costs. The wife then decided to discuss a more realistic budget with her husband. He in turn surprised her with his agreeable attitude, and he asked her why she had not brought the matter up long before. Then one day Mrs. X phoned to report with elation that a miracle had occurred. She had waited several days to make sure but wanted to report that she now slept normally and all other disturbing symptoms had vanished. The patient wrote in appreciation a year later to report the permanency of the cure. In the counseling relationship, elements of Frankl's logotherapy that entered in were the attitudinal values centering around the family organization and its limitations. The patient and counselor both shared the Christian faith with its view of the family as a " cell " of the church, and the patient was highly motivated to preserve and extend this value. The doctor in turn was aware of the patient's religious background and made his referral accordingly.

Immediately following the experience just described came another that serves to illustrate how a successful approach to personal difficulties can fail when applied to another personality whose problems are superficially similar. Mrs. X had a friend who seemed to have the same problem as she had, and which they had often discussed. In her enthusiasm she urged Mrs. Y to seek counseling. Though the situations were superficially similar, there were deeper elements here that counseling was unable to get at, and after only two consultations the client broke off the relationship in an apathetic mood that nothing could be done in her case. Perhaps logotherapy again can explain some reasons for failure here. First, enthusiasm created by the earlier success, though the miraculous element had been consciously denied, very likely distorted the necessary respect for the *individuality* of the patient, which makes him and his problems different from all others no matter how similar they may seem. This points up the need for many approaches in psychotherapy and counseling, for no one method works equally well with all clients. Secondly, Mrs. Y was not as highly motivated to face her difficulties since she had come under the pressure of a friend. A third element was that a religious outlook was lacking in the second case, and the values inherent in a Christian family organization were largely lacking. The appreciation in the first patient of the relevance of a more mature love in the presence of family difficulties, along with a decision to experiment with its effectiveness, was not matched in the second patient who had unreal and romantic expectations of love.

An analyst might explain the apparent success of counseling with the first patient in terms of transference and the casting of the counselor in the role of father figure, the authoritarian pastor whose advice one takes. The answer would be that the counselor tried to be completely nondirective, aware of the authoritarian expectations of many who come to a pastor, and further, religious values in both cases were handled only as they were brought up by the clients. The matter could also be viewed as illustrative of the " preventive medicine " that a pastor can practice through most of his ministry. This had provided a core of religious values in the life of the first patient. Through an emphasis upon the realistic meaning of Christian love as it affects all relationships, along with the significance of the family in a Christian home, the pastor can help prevent many situations resulting in disturbed personalities. This emphasis gives a positive aspect to the motivation of the individual. The approach can continually be made in sermons, educational work of the church, group activities, and all the personal relationships of the pastor with his congregation. Such pastoral emphasis helps to build a basis upon which counseling, when it is necessary, can proceed with more expectations of success, especially where short-term therapy or only one or two consultations are possible.

The high value that logotherapy places upon the singularity or uniqueness of every person in respect to himself, his vocation, " situational values " to be realized, his responsible decisions, and his choice of values can be seen as a spectrum of the general assumption of individuality made by other schools of therapy. For pastoral psychology there is a superb example of this in the way Jesus treated individuals in conversation. He never manipulated them, not even " for their own good " or for their salvation. To the contrary, the amazing variety of ways in which they found their salvation shows the keenness with which he read their individual needs. To a man " possessed of demons " (disorganized by chaotic inner forces of the id, or was it paranoid schizophrenia?) Jesus asked simply: " What is your name? " The reply indicated how accurately Jesus diagnosed the difficulty: " *My* name is Legion; for *we* are many " (Mark 5:9). The records show that he handled no other " case " in this way. To a highly moral, good, and gentle young man, who still was too concerned with his wealth, Jesus said: " Go, sell what you have, and give to the poor." He treated Zacchaeus simply as a friend and as a human being whose avarice had led him to feel like an outcast despite his wealth. No pertinent dialogue is recorded in this case, but the reality of Zacchaeus' change was proved by the opening of his pocketbook, a most acid test for any conversion. In conversation with Nicodemus, who as a Pharisee may possibly have been well-to-do but was also philanthropic, wealth was not discussed, and instead his intellectual and spiritual questions (the logotherapeutic stress on meaning) came in for discussion.

A possible complaint that Jesus was too authoritarian is refuted by an examination of the long conversation recorded in the fourth chapter of John's Gospel with the woman at the well. After several topics, Jesus came to the point of the woman's difficulty, her concern over her marriage failures and present common-law marriage. When, in possible embarrassment, the woman changed the subject to a popular religious argument, Jesus did not press the point of marriage failures, but out of respect for her as a person "nondirectively" went along. Though all details are not given, a very probable assumption is that her life too was changed by this experience in self-understanding. Though the brief interpretive sketches here may not find universal agreement among the clergy, it must be remembered that the Biblical stories are highly compressed accounts, and also that one view of inspiration allows the individual to use his imaginative capacities in reconstruction of stories involving human relationships. The pastor furthermore cannot forget that Isaiah in one of his exquisitely poetic prophecies gives the Messiah the title of Counselor.

This chapter is not a treatise on counseling, and the pedantic aim of trying to include everything has been deliberately avoided. But among the essentials, the matter of referral is particularly important because pastoral counseling has definite limitations. When a seriously disturbed parishioner needs to be referred for psychiatric treatment, the pastor should be prepared for this by an earlier established acquaintance with available doctors, psychiatrists, and social agencies.

A question that frequently arises is: "Where can we find a Christian psychiatrist?" (If a minister has to ask this, it often is because he has failed to carry out his own community responsibilities!) A realistic reply is: "Do you seek psychiatric or theological skill in your doctor?" It is small comfort, if a surgeon has bungled your operation, to know that "after all he is a good Christian." Something similar pertains in psychiatry. But the matter is not so easily disposed of by a Socratic question, for in psychiatric consultation religious difficulties as well as values often come in for treatment. Another reply is that most psychiatrists, though they may be naturalistic in their outlook, still maintain a respectful attitude toward religion and the values of the patient in therapy. An increasing number also find no incompatibility in their confession of Christian faith and the practice of psychiatry.

A related and important factor is that of the role of the pastor after referral is made and therapy started. An unfortunate occurrence that psychiatrists justifiably find lamentable is the tendency of some patients to complain to the pastor of some element in therapy. The pastor's anxieties are aroused and this leads him to denounce the therapist or his methods. The pastor's reaction then is gleefully carried back to the doctor who sometimes does not conceal his annoyance. Thus doctor and pastor are played off against each other by the patient, like a clever child who manipulates his parents, and thus he postpones facing himself in therapy. This sort of thing can be avoided by the pastor's confidence in the doctor which he has established through previous acquaintance and co-operation in community work of mutual interest.

A complete hands-off attitude on part of the pastor after he has referred a parishioner is also detrimental to the interests of the patient. He is under the necessity of "maintaining contact without splitting the transference" as Dr. Morentz has maintained.[5] The contact of the minister with the patient is the same responsibility he has toward every member of his parish except that a scrupulous avoidance of any and all forms of interference with the therapy must be maintained. After all, in hospital calling he refrains from bringing his favorite cough remedy to tuberculosis patients, and he can do the same for victims of mental disorders, while he brings both spiritual support and comfort.

In both counseling and the broader reaches of pastoral psychology, the observant pastor with some training in psychology not only practices "preventive medicine" but he occasionally is in a position to recognize symptoms of mental illness long before these would come to the attention of a doctor. The prevention of major catastrophes by trying to create more wholesome relationships also is as fine a work as the more dramatic cures of counseling or psychotherapy. Through informal play therapy a church schoolteacher discovers that an unruly problem child is reflecting a most unwholesome home environment in a family that presents a front of impeccable respectability. She can be embarrassed about this, or together she and the pastor can explore ways of meeting the greater difficulties in family relationships of which the child's behavior now is seen as a symptom. A church atmosphere, however, that is guilt and sin laden will concentrate upon the child's symptoms, belaboring him with familiar enough authoritarian devices, and using the Scriptures for horrible stories of warning, such as the bears that ate up children who were sassy to the prophet of God! The church that faces human quandries with authoritarian devices neglects the real issues of personal and spiritual development.

A certain percentage of the revulsion some psychiatrists have toward religion can be laid at the doors of fanatic clergymen whose one-sided and inflammatory preaching has created problems the therapist tries to unravel. The average churchgoer of today does not have the slightest idea of what the "unpardonable sin" is, but many patients in state hospitals still brood over the conviction that they have committed it. The relationship between this and the type of church atmosphere and preaching that reinforces the guilt and anxiety of parishioner without getting to their core, probably would be difficult to assess or survey. The Bible is very explicit in describing the callousness and unconcern of those who have committed the unpardonable sin. It follows that a person who fears he has committed it could not possibly have done so, for his sensitivity and concern are the indicators. Furthermore, the victim of this delusion usually associates it with one particular transgression or failure, whereas in the Bible the unpardonable element lies precisely in the fact that the whole orientation of the life of a person is toward callous disregard of all values and complete rejection of offered mercy. Preachers who prefer a negative approach to the gospel therefore should be experts at clarifying the Biblical meaning of sin, and relating it to the still greater Biblical emphasis upon forgiveness. Too much preaching about sin is but a projection of the preacher's own anxieties and irritations at his own guilt into the form of scolding others for their failures, while the redeeming knowledge that God has forgiven and awaits our acceptance of his acceptance is neglected.

Prof. Wayne Oates has made an excellent contribution in assessing religious factors in mental illness.[6] The "Amos complex," as one of my friends calls the practice of thundering from the Olympian heights of the pulpit, no doubt has a place in the church. But the preacher can also attempt to match it with the infinite patience of the Pastor who said: "Come to me, all who labor and are heavy-laden," and who inspired the early church to carry out in its ethos the injunction, "Bear one another's burdens." Carroll Wise feels that Jesus saw people not so much as saints and sinners but as wise and foolish. "The wise are those who respond in a positive manner and accept a fellowship which gives stability and security, even in the midst of destructive external circumstances."[7]

Most pastors would welcome a sharper delineation or division of labor with regard to their responsibilities in the counseling area of pastoral psychology. Normal human problems clearly fall within the pastor's scope, and as he develops skill in counseling and the word gets around, he can become overwhelmed with just these. The deeper clinical and abnormal problems are clearly within the province of more specialized psychotherapy, though it is not always easy to draw the line of demarcation. The pastor, therefore, needs to be well grounded in, and to keep abreast of, new developments in the area of the psychodynamics and development of the normal personality.

Gordon Allport feels that the counseling work of the pastor is complementary to the work of the psychiatrist, and "in so far as the clergy is better able to deal with issues of basic belief, values, and orientation toward life, he has an inescapable role to play in the conservation and advancement of mental health. . . . He no longer stands alone in the face of a task too great for his skill and training. He can make psychological science his ally, and share with its practitioners the solution of a problem of joint concern." [8] This function of the clergy in itself can serve to break down the lonely stereotype in which some communities would place him and which was referred to previously as " the official superego of the community."

The teaching in logotherapy concerning values as creative, experiential, and attitudinal has been discussed elsewhere in this book, but attitudinal values as realized in unavoidable suffering and in facing death have a special significance in pastoral psychology. I have also indicated earlier that the pastor has a responsibility for helping to develop more mature attitudes here. Semantic evasions and platitudes can serve to hide anxieties and doubts that will work far less harm to personality if they are more properly brought out into the open. A pastor can preach on the meaning of suffering and death without either morbid overtones or glib assurance, and can help people face their anxieties in this realm and examine their fears of what seems so fearful. Perhaps the attitude of the minister himself as he goes about this would be more important than his exact words. His tone of voice and his mannerisms as well as his choice of words would indicate to the sensitive whether or not his own anxieties about suffering or death are more prominent than his confidence in their meaning, and in God. The favorite counseling word, " acceptance," is relevant here. If the pastor can attitudinally as well as intellectually accept suffering, death, and doubts as to their meaning, seeing these as normal parts of human experience, then he can begin to draw upon the tremendous resources of God that transmute fear and anxiety into hope and energy.

Familiar enough to the pastor is a section of the Bible that runs the gamut of human emotions as men struggled with all the great issues of life — the book of The Psalms. These writings are not beautiful poetry and prayer only; they are also the passionate hammerings of men upon the anvil of God as they sought solutions to life's great problems. When they hammered long enough the psalmists discovered that they made their own souls malleable, shaped into more purposive existence by their experience. The answers they sought to their great Why? did not come in the form of neat intellectual propositions, but often enough they nevertheless achieved internal harmony or wholeness in a new dimension. Thus many a psalm begins in the minor key of complaint, but ends on a major chord of praise, because even in his distressing experience the writer found a meaning and value whose existence he had not suspected. It is this type of experience that the secular discipline of existential analysis in Frankl's logotherapy is urging modern man to consider. His appellative psychology, as he calls it in contrast to the older dynamic psychologies, appeals to the spiritual dimension of man that must be recognized in therapy if man is to reach wholeness of being. Frankl holds that if the will to meaning finds satisfying expression, then the will to power and the pleasure principle fall into proper perspective as the strivings of men whose will to meaning is frustrated.

The importance of group work is being rediscovered by the church, although in its very beginning the church was itself a movement of small groups meeting in homes, and the group emphasis has never entirely died out. A significant contribution to group therapy came about when Dr. Maxwell Jones set up his "therapeutic community" in Belmont Hospital at Surrey, England.[9] I have had the privilege of observing the work at Belmont, in addition to working with the principle as it has been applied in a large Navy hospital for several years. Its demonstrated effectiveness is impressive, and its influence now touches many hospitals. At Belmont most of the patients are social failures sent there by the courts. Despite this, an unlocked Social Rehabilitation Unit operates, where the element of trust is evident, for when given freedom and dignity these " social failures " quickly proceed to earn them. A basic ideal is the continuous striving for open and free *communication* among all members of the community, staff, and patients.

When patients learn that their ideas and suggestions are really listened to with respect, they begin to get well. Even violent psychopaths, considered " hopeless " in the scanty literature on their condition, respond to this treatment.

The implications of this for pastoral psychology are obvious if we remember that the church is primarily a redemptive community and that in some of its earliest manifestations it was highly therapeutic. One of the keys to the success of Dr. Jones's work is the freedom of communication that is always a basic goal. It is precisely here that the church often fails, right within its own organization, and in its goal in communicating its gospel to the larger community. The church staff meeting is a case in point: it can be a gathering of lackeys who are given their orders for the week by the chief of staff, or it can be an opportunity for sincere sharing, one of the true cells of the church, where each member is accorded respect for his important function and his suggestions. The governing boards of the church can be manipulated by a spiritual tyrant, or again they can operate as an effective community because each member is accepted as a person with creative capacities. The pastor can continue with these suggestions and make his own applications, for he well knows how breakdown in communications is the beginning of serious marital discord, family strife, and other failures.

The difference between a church that functions as a spiritual power in a community and one that is apathetic or strife-torn often lies in whether or not the church fails or succeeds in providing opportunities for its members to express and communicate freely their true feelings, doubts, and beliefs. So often they give lip service to the things they are expected to say and believe while inwardly torn with doubts and confusions. Certainly, if seriously ill patients in a mental hospital can be accorded the dignity and freedom of persons, learning through communication to get well and return to society with self-respect, the church can also recover these powers and function again as a therapeutic community. The work of Dr. Roy Fairchild in the Office of Family Education Research of one large denomination indicates that the church is ready to move significantly in the direction of more effective family, group, community, and cultural relationships.[10] The church whose gospel transformed whole cultures in the past has a perennial call to continue its task here.

3. Summary

This book began with an implicit question that in one way or another is treated in each chapter: What kind of man does psychotherapy propose to produce? Frankl's existential analysis was introduced as a therapy paying serious attention to the problem of human meaning. The obvious answers as these are related to the general function of psychotherapy, health, happiness, and self-realization were next discussed. It was suggested that these answers are not adequate in the light of what therapy discovers when it gets into the depths of human experience, and when it views human potentials. Therapists are realistic enough to know that they cannot guarantee health any more than Christians can learn love or fellowship by talking about them. The irony of happiness as a goal is seen in the fact that the more breathlessly we pursue, the more skillfully it eludes. Self-realization, when not related to meaning and higher values, often enough can entrap the unwary in the neurotic circle of self-idolization. These good but partial goals were seen as related to creative, experiential, and attitudinal values, and therefore the role of meaningful existence, as treated in the logotherapy of Frankl's existential analysis.

The concept of man as a central factor of importance in both psychotherapy and religion was discussed more explicitly in the third chapter of this book. Here it was urged that not only the bio-mechanistic view, but also the Christian doctrine of man is in need of reworking, particularly in the light of the contributions of naturalistically oriented research. There are indications that this already is under way in the church. Naturalistic thinkers were invited to consider the possibilities of including some of the mature thinking of the Christian centuries in their concept of man — this for the reason that Christian doctrine in its essence is always empiric. It is distilled from human experience of a transforming reality that unleashed new powers in man's life, in some cases taking the form of the profound intuitions of prophetic thinkers. The conceptual systems of Christian dogma or doctrine always followed *the event*, the experiences of man, and thus are but efforts to explain or grasp in intellectual formation what had already occurred in experience. Hence follows the emphasis on history with a goal, a purpose, in Christian thinking as contrasted to the cyclical views of Greek thought and of Spengler in our century. The actual, empiric nature of Christian concepts should not be overlooked by the naturalistic critic of religion.

In the last two chapters the intriguing possibilities of logotherapy, though applicable to all forms of psychotherapy, were discussed with reference to certain areas of counseling and pastoral psychology. Logotherapy is an open circuit which can feed into other disciplines, and it can also in turn be enriched by their insights. It does not present itself as a closed system with rigid categories and procedures, and it can serve as an invigorating stimulus in both psychotherapy and pastoral psychology. Finally, the problems touched upon were emphasized not only in their individual form as therapeutic possibilities, but also with respect to their far-reaching significance and influence upon twentieth-century culture and civilization. For what shall it profit us if we gain a whole world of therapeutic knowledge and even a lofty concept of man only to lose everything in a holocaust of international suicide? The possible destruction of our civilization or the emergence of a more idealistic culture will not result from automatic, blind "cultural forces." It will come as a result of the responsible decisions of free men, free enough to choose their values and find the meaning that a creator God has purposed for their life!

A free man, because he is free, may make himself a slave.
But a slave, because he is a slave, cannot make himself free.
                                                              — *Santayana*

APPENDIXES AND INDEXES

Notes

CHAPTER I

1. Viktor Emil Frankl, *From Death-camp to Existentialism.* The Beacon Press, Inc., 1959.

2. Marjorie Grene, *Martin Heidegger.* Hillary House, Inc., 1957.

3. See his *Grundformen menschlichen Daseins.* Niehans, Zurich, 1942. Some extended case histories written by Binswanger and illustrating the principles of his school can be found in *Existence,* ed. by Rollo May and others (Basic Books, Inc., Publishers, 1958).

4. Medard Boss, in *Psyche,* Vol. 6 (1956), p. 184.

5. In his *Theorie und Therapie der Neurosen,* Frankl discusses in detail further differences between his approach and that of Binswanger.

6. V. E. Frankl, *Theorie und Therapie der Neurosen* (Urban and Schwarzenberg, Vienna, 1956), pp. 170–171.

7. V. E. Frankl, *The Doctor and the Soul,* tr. by Richard and Clara Winston (Alfred A. Knopf, Inc., 1955), p. 124. Quotations from this book are used by permission of the publisher.

8. V. E. Frankl, unpublished lectures. January, 1959, Vienna.

9. V. E. Frankl, *From Death-camp to Existentialism.*

10. V. E Frankl, "On Logotherapy and Existential Analysis," in *American Journal of Psychoanalysis,* Vol XVIII, No. 1 (1958), p. 35.

11. Karen Horney, *Neuroses and Human Growth* (W. W. Norton & Company, Inc., 1938), p. 15.

12. This analogy is from Frankl's lectures which abound in vivid imagery, analogy, and humor.

13. J. E. Nardini gives a report of this in *American Journal of Psychiatry,* Vol. 109 (1952), p. 244.

14. Abraham H. Maslow, *Motivation and Personality* (Harper & Brothers, 1954), p. 193.

15. This still is a helpful allusion, though every schoolboy knows ostriches are too smart to hide from danger by burying their heads in the sand.

16. Dietrich von Hildebrand, *The New Tower of Babel* (Burns Oates & Washbourne, Ltd., London, 1954), p. 83.

17. Sigmund Freud, *Collected Papers* (Basic Books, Inc., Publishers), Vol. I, p. IV.

18. V. E. Frankl, from tape-recorded lectures, Vienna winter semester, 1958–1959.

19. V. E. Frankl, *American Journal of Psychoanalysis*, Vol. XVIII, No. 1 (1958), article entitled "On Logotherapy and Existential Analysis."

20. William Wordsworth, his "Lines Written in Early Spring," was composed when his revolutionary idealism was changed to horror by the cruel excesses of the French Revolution.

21. V. E. Frankl, *The Doctor and the Soul*, p. 48.

22. *Ibid.*, pp. 49–50.

23. Edith Weisskopf- Joelson, "Some Comments on a Viennese School of Psychiatry," *The Journal of Abnormal and Social Psychology*, Vol. 51 (November, 1955), p. 703.

24. E. W.-Joelson, *Acta Psychotherapeutica*, 1958.

25. V. E. Frankl, *The Doctor and the Soul*, pp. 20–21.

26. V. E. Frankl, from a paper presented at the World Congress for Psychotherapy, at Barcelona, September, 1958.

27. *Ibid.*

28. Cf. section 3 of this chapter.

29. The word "noogenic" must not be confused with the word "noetic" which Frankl uses to avoid the more religious implications of the word "spiritual."

30. Gordon W. Allport, *The Individual and His Religion* (The Macmillan Company, 1950), p. 92.

31. V. E. Frankl, *The Doctor and the Soul*, p. 280.

CHAPTER II

1. *Thoughts, Letters and Opuscules of Blaise Pascal*, tr. by O. W. Wight (Derby & Jackson), p. 160.

2. M. Grene, *Dreadful Freedom.* University of Chicago Press, 1950.

3. V. E. Frankl, *The Doctor and the Soul,* p. 63.

4. *Ibid.,* p. 73.

5. Max Scheler, *Philosophische Weltanschauung* (Bern, 1954), p. 33.

6. Karl Jaspers, *Rechenschaft und Ausblick* (München, 1951), p. 344.

7. Roger L. Shinn, *The Existentialist Posture* (Association Press, 1959), p. 25.

8. J. H. Van der Veldt, R. P. Odenwald, *Psychiatry and Catholicism* (McGraw-Hill Book Co., Inc., 1952), p. 62.

9. W. Van Dusen, *American Journal of Psychotherapy,* Vol. 114 (1957), p. 369.

10. Karl Dienelt, *Erziehung zur Verantwortlichkeit.* Österreichischer Bundesverlag, Vienna, 1955.

11. H. Johnson, *American Journal of Psychiatry,* Vol. 113 (1956), p. 36.

12. E. Lakin Phillips, *Psychotherapy, A Modern Theory and Practice* (Prentice-Hall Inc., 1956).

13. Robert M. Lindner, *The Fifty-minute Hour.* Rinehart & Company, Inc., 1955. The last chapter, "The Jet-propelled Couch," is a classic in psychiatric reporting. See particularly pp. 280–293.

14. See Vance Packard, *The Hidden Persuaders.* David McKay Company, Inc., 1957.

15. Lee Steiner, *Where Do People Take Their Problems?* Houghton Mifflin Company, 1945.

16. Paul Tillich, *The Protestant Era* (University of Chicago Press, 1948), p. 262.

17. *Ibid.,* p. 134.

18. Erich Fromm, *Psychoanalysis and Religion* (Yale University Press, 1950), pp. 86–87.

19. E. Fromm, *Escape from Freedom* (Rinehart & Company, Inc., 1941), p. 260.

20. K. Horney, *The Neurotic Personality of Our Time* (W. W. Norton & Company, Inc., 1937), pp. 264, 280.

21. V. E. Frankl, in paper read at World Congress for Psychotherapy, at Barcelona, September, 1958.

22. K. Horney, *The Neurotic Personality of Our Time*, p. 278.

23. This episode, reported in 1957 by many periodicals, tells of four young men using an airplane to penetrate the jungles, who were killed by suspicious members of the Auca Indian tribe living near their mission station. The wives of those who were married have returned to carry on the work.

24. I refer here to the well-known work of the Rev. and Mrs. Rodger Perkins, who pioneered in the use of aviation for missionary work in South America.

25. Carl Rogers, "Persons or Science, a Philosophical Question," *Pastoral Psychology*, Vol. 10, No. 92, March, 1959.

26. A layman's discussion of this is found in my *Handbook for Christian Believers* (The Bobbs-Merrill Company, Inc., 1953), Chapter II.

27. *The American Journal of Psychoanalysis*, Vol. XIII, No. 1 (1958), p. 28.

CHAPTER III

1. Max Scheler, *Die Stellung des Menschen im Kosmos* (Nymphenburger Verlagshandlung, Munich, 1947), p. 9.

2. Reinhold Niebuhr, *The Nature and Destiny of Man* (Charles Scribner's Sons, 1953), Vol. I, p. 3.

3. Sigmund Freud, *New Introductory Lectures on Psychoanalysis* (W. W. Norton & Company, Inc., 1933), p. 120.

4. Otto Rank, *The Trauma of Birth*. Harcourt, Brace and Company, Inc., 1929.

5. S. Freud, *The Problem of Anxiety* (W. W. Norton & Company, Inc., 1936), p. 96.

6. R. Niebuhr, *op. cit.*, Vol. I, p. 4.

7. Gerald S. Blum, *Psychoanalytic Theories of Personality*. McGraw-Hill Book Co., Inc., 1953.

8. Clara Thompson, *Psychoanalysis, Evolution and Development*. Hermitage House, Inc., 1950.

9. E. Fromm, *Man for Himself*. Rinehart & Company, Inc., 1947.

10. G. S. Blum, *op. cit.*, p. 31.

11. Dollard and Miller, *Personality and Psycotherapy*. McGraw-Hill Book Co., Inc., 1950.

12. S. Freud, *New Introductory Lectures on Psychoanalysis,* p. 105.

13. G. S. Blum, *op. cit.,* p. 190.

14. K. Horney, *Our Inner Conflicts.* W. W. Norton & Company, Inc., 1945.

15. Ernst Kretschmer, *Physique and Character.* Routledge & Kegan Paul, Ltd., London, 1925.

16. W. H. Sheldon, *The Varieties of Human Physique.* Harper & Brothers, 1940. Also, *The Varieties of Temperament.* Harper & Brothers, 1942.

17. Such equilibrium in bodily processes, or the maintenance of constancy of relations, has been given the name of homeostasis. Frankl's criticism of this position in psychoanalysis is contained in an article, "The Homeostatic Principle and Dynamic Psychology," in *Zeitschrift für Psychotherapie und Medizinische Psychologie* (9 Jahrgang, Heft 2, Stuttgart, March, 1952), pp. 41–47. See also his article in the *Journal of Existential Psychiatry,* Vol. 1, No. 1, 1960.

18. Pitirim Sorokin, *The Crisis of Our Age* (E. P. Dutton & Co., Inc., 1946), p. 106 ff.

19. David E. Roberts, *Psychotherapy and a Christian View of Man* (Charles Scribner's Sons, 1950), p. 95.

20. Karl Heim, *The Transformation of the Scientific World View* (Harper & Brothers, 1953), p. 131.

21. Arthur Compton, *The Freedom of Man* (Yale University Press), p. 193.

22. Martin Heidegger, *Sein und Zeit* (Max Niemeyer, Halle, 1927), p. 49.

23. D. R. G. Owen, *Body and Soul* (The Westminster Press, 1956), p. 146.

24. V. E. Frankl, "On Logotherapy and Existential Analysis," in the *American Journal of Psychoanalysis,* Vol. XVIII, No. 1 (1958), p. 33.

25. R. Niebuhr, *op. cit.*

26. C. G. Jung, *Psychology and Religion* (Yale University Press, 1938), pp. 92–93.

27. *Ibid.,* p. 95.

28. R. May, *op. cit.,* p. 71.

29. A. J. Ungersma, *Handbook for Christian Believers* (The Bobbs-Merrill Company, Inc., 1953), Chapter I.

30. Anders Nygren, *Agape and Eros*. The Westminster Press, 1953.

31. Arnold B. Come, "A New Statement of Faith," in *The Seminary Chimes*, Vol. XLIV, No. 1, p. 6.

32. E. Fromm, *Psychoanalysis and Religion*, p. 7.

33. Hans Schaer, *Religion and the Care of Souls in Jung's Psychology*. Pantheon Books, Inc., 1950.

34. *Autobiography*, Vol. II, p. 37.

35. R. Niebuhr, *op. cit.*, Vol. I, p. 14.

36. V. E. Frankl, *Logos und Existenz* (Deuticke, Vienna, 1951), p. 132.

37. V. E. Frankl, "Collective Neuroses of the Present Day," in *International Journal of Prophylactic Medicine and Social Hygiene*, June, 1958.

38. C. Rogers, "Persons or Science," *Pastoral Psychology*, Vol. 10, No. 92, March, 1959, p. 26.

CHAPTER IV

1. G. W. Allport "Scientific Models and Human Morals," in *Psychological Review*, Vol. 54 (1947), pp. 152 ff.

2. C. Rogers, "Persons or Science," *Pastoral Psychology*, Vol. 10, No. 92, March, 1959, p. 35.

3. P. Sorokin, *Social and Cultural Dynamics*. George Allen & Unwin, Ltd., London, 1938.

4. H. McArthur, *Journal of Individual Psychology*, Vol. 14 (1958), pp. 153–154.

5. Arnold Toynbee, *The Study of History* (Oxford University Press, Inc., 1947), Vol. IV, p. 263.

6. P. Sorokin, *Social and Cultural Dynamics*.

7. P. Sorokin, *The Crisis of Our Age* (E. P. Dutton & Co., Inc., 1946), p. 17.

8. P. Sorokin, *The Reconstruction of Humanity* (The Beacon Press, Inc., 1948), p. 102.

9. *Ibid.*

10. C. Rogers, *Client-centered Therapy* (Houghton-Mifflin Company, 1951), p. 49.

11. H. R. Macintosh, *Types of Modern Theology* (Charles Scribner's Sons, 1937), Preface.

12. See R. Fitch, *The Decline and Fall of Sex*. Harcourt, Brace and Company, Inc., 1957. Also, P. Sorokin, *The American Sex Revolution*. Porter E. Sargent, Inc., Publishers, 1957.

13. V. E. Frankl, unpublished lectures, January, 1959, Vienna.

14. V. E. Frankl, *Homo Patiens*. Deuticke, Vienna, 1950.

15. V. E. Frankl, *From Death-camp to Existentialism*.

16. V. E. Frankl, unpublished lectures, January, 1959, Vienna.

17. V. E. Frankl, *The Doctor and the Soul*, p. 133.

18. *Ibid.*, pp. 135–136.

19. Discussed by G. W. Allport in *The Individual and His Religion*. The Macmillan Company, 1950.

20. See W. H. Sheldon, *Psychology and the Promethean Will*. Harper & Brothers, 1936.

21. Bertrand Russell, *Power, A New Social Analysis* (George Allen & Unwin, Ltd., London, 1938), p. 11.

22. V. E. Frankl, *The Doctor and the Soul*, p. 167.

23. *Ibid.*, p. 170.

24. M. B. Arnold, J. A. Gasson, *The Human Person* (The Ronald Press Co., 1954), p. 481.

25. N. W. Ackermann, "Five Issues in Group Psychotherapy," in *Zeitschrift für Diagnostische Psychologie*, Vol. V, No. 3/4 (Stuttgart, 1957), p. 169.

26. *Ibid*, pp. 175–176.

CHAPTER V

1. Cf. John S. Bonnell, *Pastoral Psychiatry*. Harper & Brothers, 1938. Also, *Psychology for Pastor and People*. Harper & Brothers, 1948.

2. G. W. Allport, *The Individual and His Religion*, p. 77. See also Tillich's description of psychoanalysis in Chapter II, note 17, of this book.

3. Cf. Chapter III, reference 31.

4. S. Kierkegaard, *The Concept of Dread; Fear and Trembling;* etc.

5. I am indebted here to Dr. Paul E. Morentz, with whom I have discussed problems involved in making referrals. He is a practicing psychiatrist, an ordained clergyman, and teaches

pastoral psychology at the Lutheran Seminary in Berkeley, California.

6. Wayne E. Oates, *Religious Factors in Mental Illness.* Association Press, 1955.

7. Carroll Wise, *Psychiatry and the Bible* (Harper & Brothers, 1956), p. 83.

8. G. W. Allport, *The Individual and His Religion,* p. 85.

9. See Maxwell Jones, *The Therapeutic Community.* Basic Books, Inc., Publishers, 1953.

10. Dr. Roy E. Fairchild was director of the Office of Family Education Research of The United Presbyterian Church in the U. S. A., and now is professor of education at San Francisco Theological Seminary.

American Bibliography on Logotherapy

Arnold, Magda B., and Gasson, John A., *The Human Person* (The Ronald Press Co., 1954), Chapter 16: "Logotherapy and Existential Analysis."

Frankl, Viktor E., *The Doctor and the Soul: From Psychotherapy to Logotherapy*. Alfred A. Knopf, Inc., 2d, expanded edition, 1965.

——, *Man's Search for Meaning*. Washington Square Press, Inc., 1963.

——, *Psychotherapy and Existentialism*, Selected Papers on Logotherapy. Washington Square Press, Inc., 1967.

——, *The Existential Vacuum, A Challenge to Psychiatry*. The New American Library of World Literature, Inc. (in preparation).

——, "Fragments from the Logotherapeutic Treatment of Four Cases," in *Modern Psychotherapeutic Practice*, ed. by Arthur Burton. Science and Behavior Books, 1965.

——, "The Concept of Man in Logotherapy," *Journal of Existentialism*, Vol. 6 (1965), pp. 53–58.

——, "Logotherapy and Existential Analysis: A Review," *American Journal of Psychotherapy*, Vol. 20 (1966), pp. 552–560.

——, "Self-Transcendence as a Human Phenomenon," *Journal of Humanistic Psychology*, Vol. 6 (1966), pp. 91–106.

——, "On Logotherapy and Existential Analysis," paper read before the Association for the Advancement of Psychoanalysis at the New York Academy of Medicine on April 17, 1957. *American Journal of Psychoanalysis*, Vol. XVIII, No. 1 (1958), pp. 28–37.

——, "From Psychotherapy to Logotherapy," *Pastoral Psychology*, Vol. 7 (1956), pp. 56–60.

——, "Logos and Existence in Psychotherapy," *American Journal of Psychotherapy*, Vol. 7 (1953), pp. 8–15.

——, "The Will to Meaning," *The Journal of Pastoral Care*, Vol. XII (1958), pp. 82–88.

——, "The Concept of Man in Psychotherapy," paper read before the Royal Society of Medicine, Section of Psychiatry, on June 15, 1954. *Pastoral Psychology*, Vol. 6, No. 58 (1955), pp. 16–26.

——, "Group Therapeutic Experiences in a Concentration Camp," *Group Psychotherapy*, Vol. 7 (1954), p. 81.

——, guest editorial, *Academy Reporter*, Academy of Religion and Mental Health, Vol. 3, No. 5, May, 1958.

——, "The Spiritual Dimension in Existential Analysis and Logotherapy," *Journal of Individual Psychology*, Vol. 15 (November, 1959), pp. 157–165.

——, "Beyond Self-actualization and Self-expression," *Journal of Existential Psychiatry*, Vol. I, No. 1 (Spring, 1960), pp. 5–20.

——, "Paradoxical Intention, A Logotherapeutic Technique," *American Journal of Psychotherapy*, Vol. XIV, No. 3 (July, 1960), pp. 520–535.

Pervin, Lawrence A., "Existentialism, Psychology, and Psychotherapy," *The American Psychologist*, Vol. 15, No. 5, pp. 305–309. A brief review of emphases in logotherapy.

Polak, Paul, "Frankl's Existential Analysis," *American Journal of Psychotherapy*, Vol. 3 (1949), pp. 617–622.

Standal, S. W., and Corsini, R. J., *Critical Incidents in Psychotherapy*. Prentice-Hall, Inc., 1959. As a consultant, Frankl contributed to Chapters 1, 2, 3, 10, and 11.

Strunk, Orlo, "Religious Maturity and Viktor E. Frankl," in *Mature Religion*. Abingdon Press, 1965.

Vander Veldt, James H., and Odenwald, Robert P., *Psychiatry and Catholicism* (McGraw-Hill Book Co., Inc., 1952), Chapter 8: "Existential Analysis."

Weisskopf-Joelson, Edith, "Some Comments on a Viennese School of Psychiatry," *The Journal of Abnormal and Social Psychology*, Vol. 51 (November, 1955), pp. 701–703.

——, "Logotherapy and Existential Analysis," *Acta Psychotherapeutica*, 1958.

Subjects

Names